CRITICAL INTERVENTIONS IN PSYCHOTHERAPY

From Impasse to Turning Point

Haim Omer, Ph.D.

Department of Psychology
Tel-Aviv University

W. W. Norton & Company, Inc. · *New York* · *London*

A NORTON PROFESSIONAL BOOK

Composition by Bytheway Typesetting Services, Inc. Manufacturing by Haddon Craftsmen, Inc.

Library of Congress Cataloging-in-Publication Data

Omer, Haim.
    Critical interventions in psychotherapy : from impasse to turning point / Haim Omer.
        p.   cm.
    "A Norton professional book."
    Includes bibliographical references.
    ISBN 0-393-70182-4
    1. Impasse (Psychotherapy)   2. Critical incident technique.
I. Title.
    [DNLM: 1. Psychotherapy—methods.   WM 420 1994]
RC489.I45O47   1994
616.89′14—dc20
DNLM/DLC
for Library of Congress   94-12384   CIP

W. W. Norton & Company, Inc., 500 Fifth Avenue, New York, NY 10110
W.W. Norton & Company, Ltd., 10 Coptic Street, London WC1A 1PU

1 2 3 4 5 6 7 8 9 0

To my wife, Rina

CONTENTS

PREFACE

CRITICAL INTERVENTIONS are one-shot events that give a new direction to a therapy or a patient's life. Throughout the history of psychotherapy, these events have aroused curiosity, wonder, envy, suspicion, and anger. More commonly, perhaps, they have been ignored and dismissed as belonging to the realm of the irrelevant quirk or outright professional humbug; at the other end of the spectrum, they have been slavishly imitated by would-be sorcerer's apprentices. Sometimes they have become faddish, and a throng of practitioners has flocked to their source, turning the masters that coined them into gurus and their schools and clinics into shrines. Later, however, they have usually been neglected and forgotten, as one-time followers and new generations of therapists have veered back to more conventional practices or found other virtuosos to emulate. Attempts to systematize critical interventions have been scarce, for denuded of mystery they tended to lose their magic. This book is such an attempt, differing from previous ones by dealing with critical interventions *within* an ongoing therapy and not in its stead.

This difference is very significant: events that occur within a therapy still need the therapy to work them through and spell out their consequences. Furthermore, such events assume the existence of an ongoing therapeutic relationship on which their impact is based. Critical interventions are sometimes presented as revolutionary events that purport to achieve change without the underpinnings of an ongoing treatment. They are then veritable single-session therapies (Talmon, 1990), and their principles and problems are perforce very different from those of the critical interventions we shall be studying.

We shall also limit our discussion to situations in which a critical intervention is almost called for: situations of therapeutic impasse, in which the therapy's usual means and procedures get stalled. Every therapeutic approach has its own ways for understanding and handling impasse. However, as every therapist knows, impasses sometimes prove refractory even to the best that any approach has to offer. A critical intervention may then be required, as an attempt not to cure the patient at one stroke but to release the therapy from its bind.

The approach to critical interventions presented below has been developed during my work as consultant for therapeutic staffs and peer groups over the last ten years. These consultations are solution oriented: group members bring their problematic cases for discussion, expecting to get the therapies out of their unproductive ruts. The groups are heterogeneous in the psychotherapeutic orientation of their members. This variety is, as we shall see, a condition for the development of good critical interventions. In fact, the present approach could not have evolved but for today's coexistence of multiple orientations. In contrast to previous attempts at systematization, which were rooted within a specific therapeutic orientation (e.g., Alexander & French, 1946; Watzlawick, Weakland, & Fisch, 1974), the present one is clearly a child of the pluralist era (Omer & Strenger, 1992; Strenger & Omer, 1992). This brings us to an additional facet of the book. In describing critical interventions, it also presents a mirror of their natural ecology: the pluralist psychotherapeutic scene.

I owe much to the invaluable help of three persons: my wife Rina Omer, my friend Reuven Dar, and my pupil Eial Eliash. Rina and Reuven read and reread the manuscript and were extremely helpful in their comments. Eial transcribed the tapes and did the follow-ups as part of his master's thesis in psychology.

Tel Aviv, January 1994

1

IMPASSE AND

ITS RESOLUTION

PROLONGED IMPASSE IS probably the toughest and most ubiquitous ordeal of psychotherapy. We all know what impasse feels like, the doubt it casts on our sense of professionality, the lingering agony of hour upon hour of therapeutic stagnation, the anger and blame that seethe under its surface, and the oppressive thought that our long-suffering patience may cause more damage than benefit. Most therapists once believed that resistance was unavoidable, that the stuff of cure was to be found only within its knotty entrails, and that the very stiffness of the opposition reflected the value of the prize. In our skeptical era, however, we cannot but be tickled by the possibility that impasse is but an accident, the result of a mistake that should give way to a fresh approach and a new perspective, rather than an obligatory ordeal. We must face the unpleasant thought that impasse reflects not therapeutic necessity, but only the limits of our understanding and the poverty of our acts. This book is an attempt to look at impasse in this light, and to pro-

1

pose a way for developing a new perspective and formulating a *critical intervention* to release a stuck therapy from its bind.

THE DEVELOPMENT OF THERAPEUTIC IMPASSE

I shall consider three possible avenues to therapeutic impasse: (a) the therapist and the patient develop a hopeless narrative about the patient; (b) the therapeutic strategy grinds to a halt; and (c) the therapeutic relationship becomes trapped in an ineffective pattern. These three ways of getting bogged down are closely linked, as so many serial traps that are often sprung or released together.

Hopeless Narratives

According to recent views, rather than as a truth-finding odyssey, psychotherapy should be viewed as a retelling and reenacting of personal stories (Gustafson, 1992; Omer & Strenger,

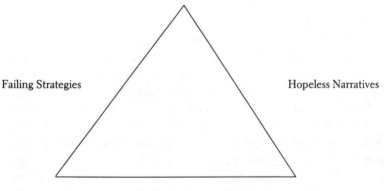

Failing Strategies   Hopeless Narratives

Ineffective Interactions

FIGURE 1   The Impasse Triangle

1992; Spence, 1982; White & Epston, 1990). Patients arrive in therapy with accounts of their lives and problems that eliminate positive options and lead inexorably to bad endings. For example: (a) people who view their lives as irredeemably split by a traumatic event before which all was beautiful and after which all is ugly; (b) people who feel so harmed by early deprivation that nothing can be good enough to make up for past ills; (c) people whose life is ruled by Groucho Marx's immortal line: "I would never belong to a club that accepted me as a member."

Successful therapy should release patients from these self-dooming narratives, an unfeasible task if therapists are themselves lured into accepting them. It is no rare occurrence, for instance, to witness a group of therapists sink into gloomy helplessness as they listen to a patient's tale of woe. A negative narrative is even harder to resist when the therapist actively interacts with the patient. A depressed person's pessimism, for instance, proves contagious, as the therapist's proposals sink swiftly and silently into a morass of nonresponsiveness. Similarly, only a strong therapist can withstand for long the inductive power of a bickering couple's mutual allegations as they vociferously trumpet their incontrovertible claims. Listening and seeing are believing and, as therapists get involved in their patients' stories, their ability to maintain an independent perspective wanes.

Therapists, however, are not just the unwitting victims of their patients' self-defeating narratives. Unfortunately, they often add their own charmed loops to make bad stories even more hermetic. Thus, child therapists who describe parents as "incapable of real love" contribute to a story in which the child must be rejected, the parents given up as lost cases, and the therapy doomed to a dead end of commiseration and resistance; similarly, therapists who attribute to their patients an ineradicable pathology turn their treatment failures into a confirmation of their own diagnosis.

Failing Strategies

It is a common experience of therapists to feel that they are pushing an apparently willing patient up against an ever steeper incline, with therapeutic results following the law of diminishing returns. Many signs harbinger the strategy's bogging down: the patient cooperates but fails to improve; new ideas are not expected to help; cooperation dwindles; previous achievements dissolve; meetings grow tiresome. Both sides seem to accept defeat without acknowledging it.

No less frustrating is the experience of therapists who try to promote a strategy that their patients openly or covertly oppose, a situation which often leads to therapeutic dropout. Sometimes, however, even this form of release fails to materialize, as patients mysteriously cling to a treatment they seem to reject.

Ineffective Interactions

The therapist's narrative and strategy may become negatively interlocked with the patient's, creating a counterproductive interaction. In a negatively complementary interaction, for instance, each side achieves the opposite of what was intended: the more active the therapist, the less so the patient; the more optimistic the therapist, the more pessimistic the patient. Complementary interactions are not merely ineffective: they may tighten the mutual grip, causing damaging entanglements that lead either to stormy separations or to "chronic" treatments that stabilize the patient's handicaps.

Ineffective interactions often develop because of negative emotional reactions on one or both sides. These reactions may lead the therapist into bad strategic and narrative choices (such as describing the patient in hopeless pathological terms or persisting stubbornly and punitively with a failing technique), and the patient into a critical or pessimistic stance. The vicious circle of negative interactions/narratives/strategies is thus perpetuated.

IMPASSE-ORIENTED CONSULTATION

Therapists can hardly be expected to diagnose and transform their unsuccessful perspectives all by themselves. We cannot but view the world through our own eyes; for a different view, we need the help of other eyes. Therefore an external consultation may prove invaluable for impasse resolution.

An external observer inevitably knows less than the therapist about the patient and the treatment and yet may be particularly able to discern new directions where none had seemed open. Less involvement allows for greater flexibility, since an ongoing therapeutic interaction creates constraints of its own. These constraints are not necessarily harmful, if the moves allowed for are such as serve the therapy. If, however, the sides settle down to a mutual appreciation and interaction that closes positive options, therapy gets stuck. Strangely, stuckness in human interactions may develop out of the very goodness of fit between the participants' motions: we learn to dance so well and so closely that each step from one partner brings a precisely matched counterstep from the other. Little room is then left for experimenting or improvising.

When impasse grows to malignant proportions, the therapy seems lost, impossible or interminable. The consultant's first goal is to map out the impasse by exploring the narratives, strategies, and interactions that create it. Sometimes all three impasse factors are found to be equally involved; at others, one seems dominant. The consultation's second goal is to design a corrective *critical intervention* to restore movement and direction to the therapy. The critical intervention stands in contrast to the routine of *normal therapy*. It aims to give therapy a jolt, release it from the impasse-producing factors and enable normal therapy to be resumed on a new basis. Impasse-oriented consultation can thus be seen to differ from regular supervision. The latter deals mainly with the right way of conducting normal therapy; impasse-oriented consultation deals with the creation of extraordinary events. To use an analogy from the philosophy of science (Kuhn, 1962), regular supervision is akin to paradigmatic science, which progresses within a generally accepted perspective; impasse-oriented consultation is akin to revolutionary science, which starts with a crisis and ends by replacing the accepted perspective.

In principle, there should be no reason why regular supervision should not also perform the job of resolving impasses. All too often, however, the supervision becomes part and parcel of the impasse, partaking of its narratives, strategies, and interactions. Furthermore, most therapists stop undergoing supervision once their period of training is over.

The consultations described in this book were conducted by me, mostly in groups. Participants were experienced psychotherapists from a variety of approaches. The consultations were audiotaped and the cases followed up by an independent investigator. The case descriptions in the book and the text of the interventions are based on the tapes and on the follow-up interviews.*

CONSULTATION AND PLURALISM

Regular supervision is usually conducted within a specific and fixed theoretical perspective. Like other forms of apprenticeship, it rests very much on a tradition of craftsmanship embodied in the school and transmitted by personal guidance and example. As long as the field of psychotherapy was clearly divided into so many mutually exclusive schools, a supervisory relationship of a unitary, continuous, and intensive character was by far the most important channel of professional formation. This state of affairs, however, was transformed by *the*

---

*The numerical data on 40 consecutive follow-ups, including the rates of implementation of critical interventions, impasse resolution, and symptomatic change, as perceived by the therapists, is presented in the Appendix.

pluralist revolution in psychotherapy (Omer & London, 1988; Omer & Strenger, 1992; Strenger & Omer, 1992).

Until recently, it was assumed that the true meaning behind any piece of behavior was unique and fixed, and that there was only one right perspective and method for unearthing and validating this meaning. A true scientific discipline should, accordingly, be free from the idiosyncracies of human judgment, reflecting instead that one true point of view. Therapy should also reflect this uniqueness: to be viewed as legitimate, it had to unearth the true and only cause of symptomatic behavior (Omer, 1989). Each school of psychotherapy (psychoanalytic, behavioral, humanistic) viewed itself as the embodiment of *The One True Theory* and *The One True Method*. Competing systems were viewed as conglomerates of superstition, shallowness, and nonsense.

In the last thirty years a series of developments in research, practice, and theory has overthrown these absolutistic premises. From 1975 on, research has repeatedly turned out *the Dodo bird's* verdict on psychotherapeutic effectiveness: all major forms of therapy seem to be effective, but more or less equally so (Luborsky, Singer, & Luborsky, 1975; Smith, Glass, & Miller, 1980). This robust finding has eroded the basis for belief in the exclusive correctness of any single existing approach.

In the practical field, the 1960s and 1970s witnessed a proliferation of new therapies, reaching into the hundreds, which led to increased give-and-take between followers of different schools. With only a few schools around, purity could still be kept, but with the emergence of hundreds of therapeutic sects mutual borrowing grew rampant: "Take my gestalt chair and lend me your family genogram." In the beginining the exchanges were made under the counter and kept away from the holy of holies of supervision. When the supervisor, however, turned the tables by proposing some unorthodox trick, everybody smiled and fraternized.

Theoretically, an assault on the schools' purity was staged by the *nonspecific factors'* approach originated by Jerome Frank (1961/1973), which seemed to describe what goes on in therapy more parsimoniously and persuasively than the specific concepts espoused by the schools. The schools' single-mindedness was further eroded by a veritable epidemic of inner skepticism, against which even their leading representatives were not immune. Thus, leading behavior therapists questioned whether their brand of therapy was really grounded in learning theory, whether it dealt with observables alone, and whether it was more scientific than other therapies (Kazdin, 1979; Lazarus, 1971, 1977; London, 1972); psychoanalysts questioned the objective truth of their own interpretations and reconstructions of the past, as well as the feasibility of the free-association method (Schafer, 1982; Spence, 1982); and cognitive therapists questioned the precedence of cognitions over emotions, the possibility of disproving dysfunctional beliefs, and even the assumption that patients' beliefs were irrational to begin with (Krantz, 1985; Mahoney, 1980; Rachman, 1980). With these developments skepticism became reputable, respect for competing aproaches grew, and the epithet "eclectic" lost its offensiveness. The emergent pluralistic order (or disorder) has no dearth of problems of its own (Strenger & Omer, 1992) but, at least for the moment, there is no way back to the lost Eden of absolute beliefs.

The present approach to impasse resolution stems from a pluralistic worldview. It tries to make a virtue of necessity by turning the very disbelief in a single approach into a therapeutic resource. One of its basic principles is that when a treatment gets stuck a radical shift in perspective and strategy may be required for overcoming the impasse. The therapeutic deadlock is released, not because the new perspective is necessarily better in any absolute sense, but because it is *different.* Not anything goes, however, and we shall see that not all solutions are equally acceptable. Pluralism and relativism are not the same as anarchy, and quality judgment is still possible without a world of fixed beliefs (Strenger & Omer, 1992). Let us begin by illustrating impasse resolution in three therapeutic vignettes.

Case 1: The Trap of Competitiveness

Miron, a 21-year-old male, had suffered a disabling accident during his military service. He was driving a jeep in a military maneuver and his commander asked him whether he could get to the top of a hill. Miron said he could, but the jeep capsized and Miron's left leg was crushed and later on amputated above the knee. Miron suffered from severe phantom limb pain, which persisted more than two years after the accident. His ambitious life plans were dashed. Before his military service, he had been highly successful in athletics. He once won third place in a nationwide competition, but having expected to win, this was a black day for him. A couple of gloomy weeks after the competition, Miron decided to broaden his athletic repertoire so as to improve his chances for the future. His mood improved as soon as he started to work hard again. In the army Miron had volunteered for the most demanding combat units. He had planned, after the army, to develop a career in athletics, perhaps becoming a sports instructor. A year and a half after the accident, Miron made a new career choice. He decided to become a pharmacist and to do it at record speed, allowing himself only six months to prepare for the highly competitive admission exams. He went to a private school to prepare for the exams and initially progressed very quickly. After a few months, however, difficulties arose, he lost his concentration, and his marks dropped. He felt that his new goal was eluding him. He stopped swimming and going to the gym and steadily increased his intake of pain-killers, which he had previously succeeded in keeping to a minimum. He became depressed and contemplated suicide. He came to therapy asking for help with his studies. The therapist, a rehabilitational psychologist, ascertained with Miron's teachers that the six-month deadline was unrealistic and that Miron was heading for a new crash.

The therapist brought the case to a group consultation three months after the beginning of treatment. The main therapeutic strategy up to then had consisted of trying to help Miron understand the unrealistic basis of his six-month deadline, the irrational sources of his competitiveness, and the dangers involved in pursuing victory at any cost. The therapist analyzed with Miron his program of studies and suggested that his goals could probably be achieved, but within eighteen rather than six months. This message was totally rejected by Miron. He blamed the therapist for trying to make him give up and told her that the sessions were increasing his depression. The therapist felt that what seemed to be the right therapeutic course was endangering the therapeutic alliance. The very mention of "moderation" drove Miron to anger and despair. On the other hand, she feared that a less direct stance, one that avoided pointing out to him what his real chances were, might be interpreted as supporting his doomed attempt.

The first task of the consultation was to analyze the narratives and strategies that were causing the impasse. The therapist viewed Miron as the victim of irrational competitiveness, while Miron viewed himself as an achiever who only needed a good push and some luck to tip the scales from defeat to victory. The two pursued opposite strategies: while the therapist spoke for moderation and tried to explore the sources of Miron's rigid drive, Miron wanted nothing but to target himself on his goal even more determinedly. These positions were locked in a hopeless complementarity: the therapist could only prevail at the expense of Miron, and vice versa.

A new narrative and strategy were developed in the course of a two-hour consultation. These are embodied in the following message, which was delivered to Miron by the therapist at the following session:

I have realized that my attitude towards you was based on a mistaken notion. I tried to help you moderate your ambitions and lower your aims, but I failed to understand that you need big challenges to feel alive. Challenges are like air for you: without them all becomes flat. Challenges led you to succeed in sports, to choose the hardest course in the army, and now, to embark on a new career. With this in mind, I hope I can tell you something wholly different and more relevant to your plight than what I've tried to tell you before.

Today you are facing what is probably your greatest challenge. You are fighting for your future, perhaps for your very life. You were forced to give up your plans and your hopes for a career in sports, and the question now is whether you will be able to find a new goal to struggle and live for. For you this is the moment of truth. Like Jacob in his fight with the angel, you are grappling with your very fate. This fight is harder and more important by far than the ones that you've faced in the past. And as I see it, in this struggle with fate you are up against something that challenges not only your will, but also your wits. The main danger is that your very fighting style may bring you defeat, for you tend to rush with all your might at any challenge that strikes the eye, but your opponent is wily and there are many snares waiting in the wings; once you rush headlong at the one that is under your nose (which you are certain to do if the snare is baited with an appetizing challenge), you will fall prey to those in the wings: growing depression, deteriorating physical condition, and addiction to pain-killers.

You've had a preview of this situation in the past, when

you came third in the athletic competition. In the begin-
ning you were depressed and thought of giving up. But
then you decided to broaden your base and go into a
variety of athletic fields. That was but a pale rehearsal of
the struggle you have today. Then you might win a medal
or not, but today your life is at stake. If you are interested,
I would like to help you in this struggle. I will tell you
about the mistakes you make, about your self-neglect in
the physical area, and about the narrowness of your plans.
You will have to broaden your base. My job will be very
different from what it was until now. I will be your coach.
I will tell you to get up earlier in the morning. You will
have to account for every pill that you take. I will help
you to plan your daily schedule, and I want you to know
that physical exercises will have to be included. Treat-
ment will be very demanding, but I think that both you
and I know full well that nothing less than all you can
give can make you face up to the present challenge.

Even before the message was relayed, the therapist felt released from her cornered position. She could now fight Miron's
self-defeating narrowness in the name of the very values that
were sacred in his eyes. She would no longer stand for patience, moderation, and resignation, attitudes that Miron de-
spised. She could tell him, for instance, that he could play the
sucker to fate if he so wanted, but that this would bring him a
silly rather than a noble defeat. The intervention dismantled
the impasse triangle by establishing a new narrative (the tale
of Miron's struggle with fate), a new strategy (the proposal of a
wider front to face the challenge), and a new interaction (mod-
eled on the relationship between coach and athlete).

Miron responded quickly. He resumed his physical exercises, reduced his intake of pain-killers and changed his daily
program so as to allow for social activities. His new catchword
was "options." Fate, however, had some aces up its sleeve:

Miron was charged with negligent driving (a long-delayed decision on the accident that had cost him his leg) and his permit was withdrawn for three months (a heavy penalty for a handicapped person); the medical board adjudicating on Miron's disability level made an absurdly low ruling and Miron had to appeal, a lengthy and time-consuming procedure; bitter fighting broke out between Miron's parents, turning the house into pandemonium. Gradually, however, Miron's optionalizing strategy achieved results and he no longer felt cornered. He was accepted by the university (though not by the coveted pharmacy department), succeeded in getting a new ruling on his handicap, and rented an apartment. Instead of the single-minded but fragile fighter that had decided to "make it" in six months, Miron had become a cool player who took disappointments in his stride.

Case 2: Bondage and Devotion

Susan was an attractive and sensitive young woman who had developed a five-year dependent attachment to a previous classmate. He would visit her about once a month, have sex with her, often with sadistic overtones, and disappear. Once he brought some friends and passed her around. He never showed her the slightest sign of respect or affection. She told her therapist that she didn't enjoy the sadomasochistic stuff, had absolutely no fantasies of that kind and had been deeply hurt by the gang sex. On the other hand, she felt she couldn't live without him, and actually came to therapy asking for better ways to keep him from leaving. Susan knew he had no love for her and that he dated other, "real," girlfriends. The thought that he might leave her made her lie in bed and meditate on his name with deep devotion until she succeeded in calming herself. She felt worthless, and her only "friends" were a few other former classmates who thought of her as a cheap girl who gave away her body for want of anything better to give.

She wrote lengthy love letters to her boyfriend, which she never showed him, rightly fearing that he would deride them.

The therapist had trouble hiding her distaste for the sadistic boyfriend and tried to strengthen Susan so that she might reassert herself in the relationship. The trouble with this strategy was that, whenever Susan dared to display the slightest assertiveness, she would become so afraid of being abandoned that she would be thrown back upon the heaviest penitential meditations on her beloved's name. The therapist felt that, rather than treatment, what Susan really wanted was a love potion. It seemed that the only effect obtained by the attempt to strengthen Susan was to make her repentance more compulsive. This impasse brought the therapist to a consultation, after four months of treatment.

Two alternative strategies were raised and ruled out by the consultation group: a paradoxical strategy of encouraging Susan's penitential rituals, based on the rationale that Susan had to reach bottom before reasserting herself; and an explorative strategy focused on the unconscious sources of Susan's masochistic inclinations. The first option was deemed personally offensive and the therapist felt unwilling to implement it. The second was ruled out because the therapist felt unconvinced that Susan had any masochistic inclinations (a feeling that was shared by all the women in the group), thinking rather that Susan had submitted to the sadistic practices without pleasure and solely out of fear of abandonment. Both strategies would probably also have met with Susan's opposition, since she denied that she derived any pleasure from the sadistic rituals and saw no constructive role (except a self-calming one) in her meditations.

A possible way out of the impasse was glimpsed when the therapist read to the group a few excerpts from Susan's love letters. If Susan's story had awakened sympathy, her letters aroused admiration. They were very special and beautiful. The following message was gradually composed, in the process of checking continuously for the therapist's, the group's, and Susan's (assumed) reactions:

> *I reread with care all the letters you gave me and I see now that we were, all along, missing a crucial point. You write again and again that your boyfriend cannot understand your feelings and that if he only could he would change his mind about you. As I read on, I slowly understood that you are engaged in a highly individual kind of creation and building up a singular quality of devotion. Emotions such as these were never expressed in this manner before. Other people have loved and suffered, maybe more than you, but your love and your suffering are special and unique. You are right in believing that he could never understand them. He would never have the patience and sensitivity to follow your images and your delicate vibrations. Perhaps only a woman could, I don't know for sure. But I think it is of the greatest importance that the two of us go over your letters, old and new, slowly and in detail, so that not a single nuance be wasted. Of course you cannot send them to him. They would be destroyed by his mere look. But I think we can both feel that you are not yearning and suffering in vain. Your grief and pain are helping you to express that very special something that lies deep within you and belongs uniquely to you.*
>
> *Let us not, at least for a while, talk about assertiveness. Instead of trying to assert yourself openly, you might develop yourself in secret, far from your boyfriend's eyes. Your boyfriend will be kept in blissful ignorance, but you and I will know all about it.*

Hours of therapy were spent over the particulars of Susan's style, imagery, and sense of drama. The letters were occasionally compared with love pieces in literature, and the two women would sometimes have a good laugh at the unwitting boyfriend's expense. Susan's bouts of separation anxiety were harnessed to the creative task, becoming tolerable in the process. Gradually, the boyfriend's stature shrank as Susan's intimate work ripened. The devotion outgrew its object. A widening chasm gaped between his fits of chauvinism and the delicacy of feeling set to writing and shared in therapy.

Susan's life began to change. She became indispensable at her job, turning into a managing secretary. Her former classmates began to recognize her worth and started meeting with her without the boyfriend's knowledge. She developed a close telephone relationship with a young man. In the meetings with the boyfriend, an impish streak became manifest: five minutes after having sex, she would want more. The boyfriend could not fail to respond and would gather all his male prowess to meet the challenge. Five minutes later she would feel sexy again.

About eight months after the consultation, Susan was still meeting with her boyfriend once every two or three months, but she now felt comfortable with the long intervals and would sometimes cancel a meeting if it proved too close for her taste. She now viewed the relationship as purely sexual. She stopped writing about him, no longer thought that she was in love, and felt no anxiety when he failed to contact her. She was eager to develop an attachment of a different kind, but was strangely bashful with other men. The therapist told her that this showed how inexperienced she was in mutuality, and that being caressed and kissed with affection would seem much like first-time events. Susan was very intrigued by these remarks.

Case 3: A Problem of Self-Esteem

Dora's therapist started the consultation by saying she wanted to present a problem of self-esteem. Dora was 35 years old, married to a painter and mother of a son and a daughter. Though highly respected by her colleagues (she practiced law in a highly reputed office), by her friends, and most of all, by her husband, Dora worried constantly about the impression she made and about her lack of worth. The respect and admiration she received were no indication, to her mind, of her real worth, because most people are ready with praise. Her husband's appreciation, in particular, she dismissed with a wave of her hand. Esteem from the precious few who really counted was not easily forthcoming, and when it came she found ways of either discounting it or downgrading the admirer. She was highly critical of herself and imagined that people with judgment could only evaluate her as she herself did. She worried so much that life became a continual struggle. She only experienced respite when alone or when traveling abroad on her own. She would signal the special comfort she felt during these trips by brief extramarital affairs. At home, she felt exhausted and frustrated by the endless tension.

She had undergone three years of psychoanalytic therapy in which her lack of self-esteem was traced back to her family of origin and in particular to the facts that her elder brother, now a physicist, had easily earned the crown of "family genius," and that in her parents' opinion "a woman could never really make it." Dora followed the family tradition by feeling good about her son's achievements but being critical of her daughter's. However, the previous therapy had failed to improve her preoccupation with her own worth. If anything, she felt even more obsessed, a conclusion that was endorsed by her husband. Dora asked for a short, practical treatment, feeling that she had had enough of understanding herself.

After seven sessions, the therapist felt stalemated by Dora's disqualifying moves. Attempts to help Dora develop inner sources of respect were stalled by her high-handed dismissal of support or appreciation. Attempts to explore the sources of her problem met with a similar fate: Dora would say that her previous therapist had tried long enough to make her feel like "a lovely baby deserving to be admired just for being so cute." Attempts to empathize with her pain, present or past, were dismissed by a roll of the eyes or a shoulder shrug. All the therapist's reserves of Kohutian sensitivity seemed unable to sound the bottom of Dora's sense of hollowness.

The group's response initially echoed and amplified the feeling of paralysis. Participants recalled cases they had tried to treat but in which the basic lack had been so profound as to be all but irremediable. Pessimistic interpretations were bandied about, and the participants seemed launched on a competition for who would offer the most insoluble pathogenetic perspective or trace the deprivation to its earliest level. The group had become trapped in the same impasse that was plaguing the treatment. It seemed that conceptualizing the problem in terms of a deficit in Dora's sense of self was counterproductive. As the group groped for an alternative description, someone asked how people from other times or cultures would have described a person like Dora. This question shifted the focus onto other aspects of Dora's behavior, such as her disrespect and infidelity towards her husband, her tendency to dismiss others, and her need to place herself only with the highest strata of humanity. Dora was redescribed as a supercillious aristocrat of the mind. This rather unpsychological characterization proved more productive than the former, leading to the following intervention:

> You are right in thinking that another lengthy, explorative therapy would probably do you little good. But maybe what I am going to tell you will not look like therapy at all. I believe that you really have a flaw, a spiritual flaw. Your flaw is the the sin of pride. This might seem strange to you, as you don't feel proud of yourself at all. The sin of pride, however, is a deeper thing. It consists in worrying oneself constantly about one's stature as compared to that of others, in disparaging the low and their

*opinions, or in being so overawed by the great that noth-
ing counts so much as being admired by them. You are
obsessed with pride. You look upon life vertically, as a
gradient of worth, and cannot accept the fact that you
don't see yourself at the top. There are two kinds of situations that persons suffering from the sin of pride cannot
handle: when others do not appreciate them, and when
others do appreciate them. The first leads you into a spi-
ral of self-denigration and despair, the second into a spate
of discounting reactions, either showing the appreciation
to be unfounded or the appreciators unworthy. The sin
of pride carries its own punishment, dooming you to go
round and round with never a hope for satiation or fulfill-
ment, with just a minimum of relief when you are alone,
or away.*

*In all cultures there has always been one antidote to
the sin of pride: self-abasement. If you want change you
will have to learn to mortify your overblown self, to starve
your appetite for admiration, to fight your arrogance. You
need a good self-abasing routine for those times when
you feel worried about success and about how others will
react to you. If you want to improve your self-esteem,
there is nothing that I can do. Your true enemy, however,
is pride. It contaminates all in your life, your relationship
with your husband, your daughter, your friends, your
peers. You were right in feeling that sympathetic support
is not what you need in therapy. Neither do you need further examination of what you underwent as a child. You
knew that you wanted stronger medication, and this is the
line that I think we should follow in our brief therapy.*

In sharp contrast to her usual behavior, Dora hardly said
a word, and the dismissive eye-roll and shoulder-shrug were
conspicuously absent. Immediately after the session she wrote
a detailed confession of her arrogant manners and disparaging

thoughts. She showed it to a childhood friend, to whom she also described the puzzling therapeutic message. Her friend corroborated the therapist's judgment and the confession, telling her that people had always stood in great fear of her biting sarcasm. The therapeutic interaction changed: Dora stopped obsessing about her worthlessness, talking instead about how to improve her relationship with her husband and children. A few sessions were devoted to an attempt to correct the vicious circle in which Dora had become stuck with her daughter. After three months she told the therapist that her self-worth preoccupations seemed so puny that she could hardly understand how her life had been ruled by them. She terminated therapy, having for the first time in years planned a trip abroad with her husband.

THE IMPASSE-RESOLUTION MODEL

The model of impasse sketched above postulates a confluence of three factors: a negative narrative, a failing strategy, and an ineffective interaction. The critical intervention is an attempt to change this threesome nexus. Let us examine the case illustrations for how the factors were interrelated and addressed.

In Miron's case, both sides initially held diametrically opposed versions of what was going on: the patient felt that all he needed in order to succeed was to try harder and get a good push, whereas the therapist believed that the very attempt was destructive. The incompatibility of these views made for an ineffective therapeutic strategy (aimed at moderation) and for a negative complementarity: the therapist's attempt to help was driving the patient to anger and despair. The critical intervention changed the narrative by adding a new character, "Fate," which was cast as the wily adversary that changed the rules but made the game all the more worthwhile. The new therapeutic strategy did not differ from the old so much in content as in name: in both cases the therapist encouraged the patient to broaden his base and open new options, but this line was presented previously as a strategy of patience and resignation and now as a way of playing a better game; previously, the patient had been exhorted to be "less competitive," now, "not to be a sucker." This narrative reformulation transformed the strategy and the interaction: therapist and patient were now on the same side, trying to outdo Fate.

In the second case, the therapist's attempts to make Susan more assertive led only to ever starker proofs of self-abnegation. Instead of encouraging Susan to withstand her boyfriend, the new strategy helped her to look at herself in the wondrous mirror of her devotion. The original narrative line attempted to follow the pattern of "The Karate Kid," in which the victimized weakling is coached towards a fateful confrontation; the new narrative followed the pattern of "The Ugly Duckling," in which the victimizer is not beaten but belittled. The negative complementarity by which assertiveness training had led only to more self-abasement was loosened when the therapist chose to avoid confrontations with the boyfriend.

In the third case, a story about "lack of self-esteem" was transformed into one about "the sin of pride," and a supportive strategy was changed into a confrontative one. The therapeutic relationship, which had become stuck in the Sisyphean task of trying to fill in the abysmal lack in Dora's sense of self, improved immensely once the therapist chose to focus on Dora's flaws. The negative complementarity in which self-criticism had been followed by bland encouragement was dismantled once the therapist dared to confront Dora's aristocratic aspirations with deeper values.

In all three cases the critical intervention enabled the therapist to respond differently to a possible resurgence of the impasse. In the first case, a reappearance of Miron's narrow self-targeting could be challenged by telling him that he was again playing into his opponent's hands; in the second, if Susan's yearnings for her boyfriend reappeared, they could be channeled into the secret work of devotion; in the third, a return of the self-worth obsession could be met by telling Dora that pride was trapping her again. The interventions thus fortified the treatments against possible recurrences of the original problem.

The actual treatment messages cannot be deduced directly from the bare outline of the impasse model. There is a conceptual leap between the triangle of impasse and the specific ideas and words that constitute the critical intervention. The rest of this book is an attempt to clarify this conceptual leap and turn the construction of critical interventions into a craft rather than an inspirational flight.

A word of caution: critical interventions may fail. The therapist may choose not to implement the intervention; the patient may be unaffected by the message; or even more frustrating, the therapist may implement the message and the patient may seem to accept it, but with no resulting change. Sometimes, as we shall see, failure serves as the occasion for a further intervention. Sometimes we are left only with the story.

2

THE IMPACT OF

CRITICAL INTERVENTIONS

FROM ITS VERY BEGINNINGS, psychotherapy has been intrigued with the moment of change. The abreactive surge, the flashing insight, the sudden return of lost memories or, more recently, the breakdown of long-standing avoidances are almost stereotypical images of therapy's crucial moments. Such breakthroughs are viewed as attainable only by pitting the most determined and unswerving efforts against the patient's obstinate resistance. When these hoped-for events occur, their emotional intensity serves as virtual proof of the therapeutic method by which they were evoked. Not only therapists, but also writers and, most of all, the cinema have turned the dramatic psychological breakthrough into a cultural symbol of almost mythical proportions. And yet, a closer look at moments of therapeutic change, in particular when they occur after a lengthy period of apparent stagnation, suggests a different picture. The breakthroughs described in Standal and Corsini's (1959) classic *Critical Incidents in Psychotherapy*, for instance, seem to result not from the therapists' grim tenacity in pursuing their course but from their readiness to act differently, sometimes scandalously so, from how they were wont to. It seems that, rather than proving their dauntless devotion to the One True Method, therapists who succeed in resolving impasses tend to react to them by changing gear and breaking their own rules.

This perspective on critical interventions in therapy has been encapsulated in a well-known formula by the authors of *Change* (Watzlawick, Weakland, & Fisch, 1974): *Never do more of the same.* Today, two decades after the book's appearance, we are growing aware of the formula's limitations as well as its power. For how do we know that enough of "the same" has been attempted and that a new approach is needed? Are there not situations in which "the same" has been applied so half-heartedly that implementing it in a more determined way, with closer attention to loopholes and leakages, would make "the same" different? Sameness is a hazy matter: different people see different similarities, and resemblance is the shade of difference. Some people see impasse where others see slow progress, and where some feel the need for a bang others make do with a whisper.

Impasses and critical interventions are thus, in the final analysis, a matter of personal judgment. Some therapists are gradualists, believing that valuable achievements can only be achieved by painstaking processes that slowly undo what a bad past did; others are radicalists, assuming that change is a steep step function. The present approach leans, on the one hand, toward radicalism: it is suspicious of "very slow progress" and views stagnation as an injurious rather than a harmless waste; on the other hand, it partakes of gradualism, viewing the critical intervention as a trigger that requires ongoing normal therapy to make good on the shifts sparked by it. The critical intervention serves as a transitional event, a switch, a rite of passage. To this end, it must have a powerful impact on patients' minds, impinging on their awareness and remaining there as a salient signpost dividing what went on before it from what is to come after it.

THERAPEUTIC IMPACT

To be effective therapeutic interventions must overcome the tendency to disregard them. A patient may, for instance, not pay attention to the therapeutic message or do so only perfunctorily so that the rules of politeness are kept. If the therapist succeeds in capturing attention, the patient may yet water down the message by carrying out its meaning only in a careless manner. Patients' slack performance of therapeutic tasks, which often gives the impression of willful sabotage, actually may only reflect the small amount of mental space allotted to the therapist's messages amidst the many demands of daily life. Even when the therapist succeeds in being heard, a process of habituation may slowly creep in, so that with each new session the therapist is more and more taken for granted, blending with the background. A therapeutic message may also lose power by being accessible only in the quiet of the treatment room, being pushed aside once a demanding situation arises. Treatment is thus all but insulated from the problem area where it should make itself felt. Inattention, neglect, habituation, and insulation are only some of the ways by which therapeutic effects are dissipated. With time, the erosion of long-term forgetfulness and the inertia of old habits take their toll.

The concept of *therapeutic impact* refers to the power of an intervention to overcome these many varieties of disregard (Omer, 1987, 1990, 1992). It implies that therapy may prove ineffective not only, or even chiefly, because of deep pathology or intractable resistance, but simply by failing to make an impression strong enough to compete with life's demands. Therapy has but a short hour of grace to make itself felt against the endless barrage of stimuli that call for attention and energy every minute of every day. Little wonder, then, that if thera-peutic messages are not relayed with the greatest power, they are doomed to be washed away.

These various obstructions to therapy have usually been dealt with under the concept of resistance. Resistance, how-ever, implies unconscious (or conscious) conflicting motiva-tion, whereas the concept of impact implies mainly passive processes, such as a natural tendency to save energy or a lim-ited capacity for processing information. Motivated resistance certainly plays a role in therapy and the literature is rich in ways for dealing with it. The passive processes by which ther-apy gets wasted, however, have been largely neglected.

To achieve impact, one must first of all make sure of *the patient's positive attention*. Watching outstanding therapists at work, we can see that, far from taking the patient's attention for granted, they cultivate it assiduously, promoting expectan-cy, creating suspense, establishing a clear focus, and stressing the special status of important messages. Mere attentiveness is not enough, however, as shown by many a paranoid patient who listens eagerly to all signs emitted by the therapist only better to reject or misconstrue them. What is needed is a state of *positive* receptiveness. Therapists must therefore make sure also of their emotional ground, which they do by joining moves and empathic statements that convey reassurance and support, or by building on urgency and persuading patients that they cannot afford to remain indifferent.

The next foundation of therapeutic impact is the appro-priate use of *emotional arousal*. Therapists need powerful emo-tions not only because they are the stuff of personal change, but also because they make therapeutic events memorable. We remember well our moments of deep feeling, endow them with special significance and turn them into signposts in our life journey. The story of a therapy, too, is often viewed in retro-spect as unfolding from a highly emotional event. The more quiescent periods are often interpreted as either preparatory to the emotional climax or as a working through of its achievements.

Another major impact role is played by *specialness and surprise*. The quaint atmosphere, the unusual episode, the counterexpectational twist, and the paradoxical turn are gradually becoming respectable tools of the trade. Patients, as all sentient organisms, habituate quickly. The weekly or biweekly therapeutic hour may become part of the routine that helps to keep life uniform and stable. August is for such patients the cruelest month, when, due to the absence of their guarantor of sameness, uncalled-for personal adventure may strike. For the therapist who feels uncomfortable as a protector of the status quo, the extraordinary therapeutic event may be an appropriate antidote. Such a therapist must, however, beware of addicting patients to the exceptional, for patients may become so acclimatized to therapeutic shocks as to require them in each and every session.

Commitment and mobilization to action can also make the difference between an intervention that is doomed to oblivion and one that leads to productive change. We remember well what we work hard to achieve. The very act of self-commitment creates impact, making us allocate mental space to the task at hand. Therapeutic action, furthermore, should impinge directly upon the life-area where the problem is felt. It is vital to *establish contact between the therapy and the problem*, so as to avoid the insulation of therapeutic messages within the confines of the therapy room.

Some formal characteristics of the therapeutic message itself, and of the way in which it is relayed, also carry impact. The judicious use of *vivid words and images*, for instance, is a quasi-literary therapeutic skill that is seldom taught in therapy schools (Omer, 1993b). A message couched in vivid terms strikes deeper than one framed in hazy or abstract ones, and a good therapeutic catchword reverberates in the mind, compressing many long-winded therapeutic insights. *Rhythmic or* *varied repetitions* of therapeutic messages, if pursued with care, can also add to an intervention's lasting power. Patients occasionally tell of the persistent echo of therapists' words in their ears, and the right sound may be as important in this respect as that of a good commercial jingle. The *convergence of different themes* into one therapeutic accord may cause a strong imprint, especially if it also brings about a confluence of emotions and motivations. A subsequent reappearance of one of the themes will then serve as a reminder of the others, modifying and enriching the therapeutic dialogue.* *Perceptual and conceptual contrasts* also lend memorability to messages. Out of an array of possible stimuli, our mind seems wired to pick up contrasts, utilizing them to organize the welter of incoming data. The little that has been written on these formal characteristics of therapeutic communications has tended to relegate them to the realm of therapy's ineffable artistry. As I hope to show, far from being necessarily so, formal principles for the creation of enduring messages can be clearly enunciated as in any respectable craft.

The factors listed above do not exhaust the many ways by which therapists prepare their ground and endow their messages with staying power. Even this partial list, however, has been shown capable of accounting for the differential effectiveness of therapeutic interventions (Omer, Dar, Weiner, & Grossbard, in press; Omer, Kadmon, Wiseman, & Dar, 1992). These findings suggest that, at present, the formation of therapists may be incomplete. We are taught to listen to the patient, to attend to the therapeutic relationship, and to consider the contents of our communications. We should also learn, however, to take care of impact, for we are, willy-nilly, dramatists for an audience of one.

---

*The integration of different messages into one integrative focus is taken up in detail in Chapter 6.

The best analysis of impasse may go to waste if it is not incorporated in a high-impact intervention. In the examples below we shall focus, therefore, on impact-promoting means, leaving the issues of narrative reconstruction, strategic change, and interactional repair to the following chapters.

Case 4: Little Rascal or Criminal?

Gil was an 11-year-old boy who played truant from school, cheated, stole from stores, from other kids and from his parents, beat up his nine-year old brother almost daily, and came home later and later every night. The boy seemed refractory to discipline or persuasion. The mother, who made the appointment, was deeply distressed and in despair, but the father seemed satisfied with Gil, thinking him extremely smart. Being Gil's father was great fun because it was an equal fight: Gil tried to outsmart him and he outsmarted Gil in turn. When asked for examples of Gil's smartness, the father gave the following one: two days after receiving his weekly allowance, Gil complained that he had lost the money and whined so piteously that they ended up giving him a new allowance. In fact, the parents knew all along he had not lost the money, but only when the grocer told them that Gil had recently bought lots of sweets with ready cash did they give up the pretense of having been duped by the fib. Gil's "smartness" was also shown at school when his teacher sent him to the principal because he had arrived late for three days in a row. Gil went to the principal but from there went straight home without returning to his class. When called to account, he said that the teacher had not told him that he had to go back to class. The father applauded, and the mother, sheepishly, agreed.

In the father's opinion, the best way to prepare Gil for life was to fight him at his own level, by outsmarting him again and again. He wanted the therapist to help him in this task.

The mother, on the other hand, complained that the father was very impulsive. On a whim, he would check on Gil's homework and, finding that Gil had no idea what it was, would beat him up and decree a severe punishment (a month's grounding, for instance) that the mother would be unable to implement. The mother believed that Gil should be reached by love and kindness, but she did not know how to do it. She felt unable and unwilling to set and enforce demands.

In a couple of individual sessions, Gil told the therapist that he had many friends who were actually his "agents," and with whom he planned how to steal sweets and toys, bamboozle teachers, and cheat other kids ("the suckers"). He described with relish how he cheated his brother (described by the parents as the perfect child) in Monopoly, and how he "murdered" and "tortured" him for any provocation, real or imaginary.

The mother decided to ask for help after an incident in which Gil had been forbidden to go to a party because of some mischief he had committed. Gil ran away. The father looked for him in his car, where Gil would sometimes hide, but failing to find him there, chose not to look for him at his friends' so as not to be taken for someone with no control over his son. Gil did not return until the next morning. The father convinced the mother to play it cool so as not to fall into Gil's trap by appearing worried. This they did, but the mother was quite shattered by the experience.

In the course of three sessions with the parents, two with Gil, and one with the whole family, the therapist tried unavailingly to develop a constructive therapeutic strategy. Gil wanted only to brag about his exploits. The mother had all but given up. The father trusted the "little rascal," and said that when he was a kid he had behaved exactly the same. Straight talk with the parents about rules, goals, and sanctions fell on deaf ears. The therapist felt she had no grip upon the slippery surface of the parents' attitudes. The following critical intervention was developed in consultation in order to jolt the family from their apparent satisfaction (father), giving-up (mother), and nonconcern (Gil).

The therapist was to call the parents and make a special appointment for the whole family in which they would be given a summary of the intake's conclusions concerning Gil's problem. They were told that all four had to be present, that the summary would be delivered orally and in writing, and that the session would be very short. When the family arrived, each member was given a personal envelope with the same letter, which was also read aloud by the therapist:

There is a riddle in your family calling for a solution. The riddle is: why must Gil become a criminal? Or, more precisely, why must Gil become a criminal of a very special type, the jailbound criminal? For Gil is clearly developing the habits of a jailbound criminal, and you, father and mother, are unwittingly helping him to become a jailbound criminal by pretending to be suckers. For instance, you allow Gil to cheat you about the weekly allowance and you behave as if you believed him, whereas in reality you do not. It is very strange, for instance, that you pretend to be suckers, as when you decide to punish Gil by not allowing him to go out, while you know very well that he may run away. So why do you do this? And why do you play the suckers when Gil stays out for the whole night, pretending the next morning that it didn't bother you? Why is it that, when Gil lies, steals, destroys, and bullies others you two say that he is smart, roguish, daring, and wild? For of course you know full well that he is not actually just wild, daring, roguish, and smart, but that he bullies, destroys, steals, and lies. Of course, when you do this, Gil doesn't learn how to protect himself. He learns, instead, to believe that the world is full of suckers like his parents. This will surely land him in deep trouble. The riddle is, why do you do this? And why does

Gil, who sometimes seems smart, agree to take part in this make-believe? Why does Gil fall into the trap and foolishly believe he has outsmarted you, when obviously he hasn't?

The riddle is a difficult one, because no one likes to sit in jail for many years, yet Gil behaves as if this were his goal in life and you, his parents, behave as if you agree with this goal. But this is not true. You both worry about him a lot and surely wish for a good and healthy family, rather than one with a kid in jail. So why is this so?

Maybe, Gil, you decided, without knowing, to sacrifice yourself in becoming a jailbound criminal. But for whose sake are you sacrificing yourself? Who stands to gain from your training to become a jailbound criminal? Of course, your brother Adam stands to gain because when one of the brothers is black, the other automatically turns out white. If you train yourself to become a jailbound criminal, Adam will probably become a successful man. Thus, your sacrifice is not in vain. Still, it is hard to believe that you are doing this for his sake, particularly as you enjoy beating him up so much. So the riddle remains.

Is there any other good that comes out of your behaving as a jailbound criminal? You two, father and mother, are united by this issue. You are both united in your concern about Gil. In our meetings I can see positive things between you two, a special closeness, the closeness of common concern. But this hardly solves the riddle, for Gil would not sacrifice himself just to make you worry together.

Sometimes, Gil, it seems you get a little fed up with being a jailbound criminal and would like your parents to stop pretending. For instance, when you stayed out the whole night, I think you would have liked your parents to have reacted otherwise, so as not to allow this ever to happen again. But you failed. They continued to pretend. Well, this was in any case exceptional, because most of the time you seem satisfied with training for a jailbound criminal.

And what about you, Adam? You get beaten up pretty often by your brother. At least you can find consolation in the fact that each slap and kick makes you detest more and more the ways of jailbound criminals, so that you will surely not become one.

Only the two of you, father and mother, can decide whether to continue in the role of despairing parents or to try other options. Without strength and hope, maybe it is best to accept Gil as he is, acknowledge the price you are paying, give up, say Kadish* over him, and direct the energy that is left to other issues.

The family was not allowed to discuss the letter and only the parents were invited for the next session. The therapist was coached by the group on how to avoid negative complementarity in the future: if the parents reacted once again to interventions with declarations of helplessness or nonconcern, she should go back to an exposition of "the family riddle." By no means should she respond to the parents' passive complaining and helpless stance by offering suggestions or directives. For instance, if the parents complained about Gil's cruelty to Adam, the therapist might counter that there was some ironic justice in the situation, for Adam, like tempered iron, was getting stronger with each beating; if the father showed pride in Gil's cheating, the therapist could ask him whether he had really been fooled by Gil's naïve ploys or only pretended to be; if the mother whined helplessly, the therapist could ask her whether, at least, having despaired of Gil made her better able

---

*The traditional Jewish prayer for the dead.

to devote herself to other tasks. The therapist was, however, to show approval and support for solutions the parents initiated and help them elaborate upon them. This became the central line of the new normal therapy.

The impact of this intervention was secured by a variety of means. To make sure the family members were attentive, the message was to be delivered in a quasi-ritualistic manner: the parents were told that an important communication would be delivered, orally and in writing, in a very short session that had to be attended by all family members. Such an extraordinary session would stand out conspicuously among the previous and following ones.

The message made use of evocative expressions and images such as "jailbound criminal" and "saying Kadish." Besides these singular epithets, it was couched throughout in stark terms such as "suckers," "lying," "stealing," "destroying," "sit in jail," "despair," and "give up," which were designed to dismantle the family's self-soothing mechanisms.

The message was further hammered home by a piling up of questions and a judicious use of rhythmic repetitions: "jailbound criminal" and "suckers," for instance, reverberated throughout the intervention. More subtly, the sequences "lying, stealing, destroying, and bullying" and "smart, roguish, daring, and wild" were mutually contrasted and repeated twice in reversed order. The aim of this word pounding was to counter the parents' preference for endearing or minimizing terms for Gil's misdemeanors, so that any future use of these terms would evoke also their harsher counterparts. The family's whitewashing habit was thus therapeutically "contaminated." Patients who are exposed to such a procedure often react with a shamefaced smile when, in subsequent sessions, they slip again into their prettifying terminology.

Impact was also enhanced by shocking the family into a sense of urgency. A preview of Gil's future as a jailbird was appended to his description as a "jailbound criminal." This was followed by an explicit exoneration of the parents from any imputation of negligence which might have estranged them.

The paradoxical use of the theme of Gil's "self-sacrifice" in favor of his brother also played a role, for the surprising is remembered better than the expected. Smart kids can see through such uses of paradox and often pooh-pooh them quite openly in the session. It is quite common for a child who lives in an atmosphere of trickery to expose the ploy with a triumphant: "Ha! You tell me that when I beat him up I am actually helping him and sacrificing myself for him, only to make me stop beating him up!" Such a "discovery" does not necessarily invalidate the intervention, particularly if the therapist refrains from behaving defensively. A good response might be: "I would surely be glad if you stopped beating your brother as a result of what I said. But if you don't, just pay attention to the results of your beatings. At home, he and your parents will become more and more convinced that he is in the right. At school, or with friends, he will be only the happier because he is far from you, so that he will become more pleasant and friendly. Whatever you may think, your beatings cause him pain, but they also make him look better."

Impact was further served by mobilizing the parents for action in an indirect manner. The mention of "other options" in the message's final clause, though left undefined, would motivate new parental behaviors, since the alternative ("saying Kadish") was quite unacceptable.

The intervention's role as a transitional event in the therapy was signaled by the therapist's singular refusal to discuss the message in the session and her further avoidance of any directive role. By refusing to discuss the message, she aborted the family's typical ways of eroding and dismissing therapeutic communications by endless objections and mutual bickering. By her systematic avoidance of a directive role, she marked the shift from therapy as guidance to therapy as provocation and support.

The parents' immediate reaction showed that a new chord had been struck: they listened almost in awe and left the room without comments. On their way home, Gil raved about the "disgusting woman" who had called him a "jailbound criminal." For a month, he tried to prove her wrong by behaving as the ideal child. The mother, though initially skeptical, gradually began to believe that Gil was capable of behaving differently. Thereupon, she became more willing to make demands and rules, and to stick by them.

A month later, Gil stole money from his mother and threw a smoking party with some kids from his class. Two of the boys felt remorse and told their parents about it. Gil's mother (who had suspected Gil of stealing but had not been sure) was called to the school. Gil, as usual, lied brazenly before the principal (rather stupidly, as the case against him was clear-cut), but the mother reacted in a new way. She took Gil home in silence and, once home, told him peremptorily that he was not to leave his room until she had talked things over with father. The matter was too grave to be judged on the spur of the moment. The parents decided that Gil would stay in his room for the weekend and this time they took steps to enforce the punishment. Gil seemed rather intimidated and made no attempt to challenge them.

The father still tried to play down the importance of what had happened and said he was impressed by how Gil had held his own before the principal. The therapist was very curious about his being so impressed, for Gil had been caught thrice over in his act (by two of his mates who complained and by the mother who suspected) and nobody had been convinced by his lies. The father agreed sadly and, for the first time, confessed that he had been quite different as a child. This confession proved to be the turning point in the father's relationship to Gil and to the therapy. The therapeutic-parental system was now better prepared for crises.

Case 5: Propitiating the Gods*

Solly, a medical student, suffered from a compulsion to touch and align almost every single object in his flat before going to sleep. Some activities he had to perform in very special ways, such as touching the key four times when locking his door, failing which he had to step up to the next multiple of four, and so forth. These and other rituals could take up to eight hours a day. Any neglect on his part would lead to overwhelming fears of certain catastrophe. A mysterious agency, immune to all rational arguments, seemed to hover malignantly over his life. Solly asked for practical help with this problem and was initially uninterested in exploring other aspects of his life. He had chosen this particular therapist because of his reputation for focused problem-solving. The therapist, accordingly, started on a program of gradual exposure with response prevention, aided by self-control techniques. There was little progress, however, for Solly usually gave up at the very first signs of anxiety.

After a while, possibly as an escape from the anxiety-provoking homework, Solly expressed interest in exploring broader issues. He complained of feeling ruled and "preprogrammed" by his mother, to the point of not knowing what his own wishes and desires were. For instance, any girl he dated had to be checked against his mother's list of obligatory attributes (beauty, property, good family, correct ethnic and cultural background, aesthetic taste, polished manners, and right attitude toward prospective mother-in-law), a procedure which nipped all relationships in the bud. The therapy began to veer in this new direction, but then Solly complained that his examinations were coming up and his compulsions were becoming unbearable. Therapy seemed doomed to fruitless oscillation. A

*A shorter version of this case appeared in Omer, 1993a.

message and an ordeal were then devised to channel this pendular movement in a productive direction:

> *In your touching behavior you describe a feeling of being*
> *always intent on placating the gods, failing which you*
> *fear you will be punished by all manner of catastrophic*
> *events. Feeling that you don't own your life, you must*
> *have recourse to propitiatory rites to appease its rightful*
> *owners. These gods are very similar to your mother,*
> *whom you try to placate by making all the right choices.*
> *In fact, the compulsions and the dependent relationship*
> *with your mother are the two sides of the same problem:*
> *in both you behave as the abject worshiper of oppressive*
> *deities. In learning to fight the compulsions, you will*
> *therefore become able to face your mother and discover*
> *your own wishes; and in learning what you really want*
> *and daring to face your mother, you will find yourself*
> *fortified against the compulsions.*

Solly was very much taken with this formulation and asked
the therapist if there was anything of an immediate nature
that could be done about his symptoms. The therapist told
him that he had in mind a task that would surely advance him
considerably in the right direction.* It would be a hard task,
but one which Solly would be able to perform. The therapist
would disclose the task, however, only if Solly were to give,
beforehand, his total, unconditional commitment to undertake
it. Solly pledged himself. The therapist then instructed him to
buy ten pounds of honey and put it in a big pot under his bed.
Before going to sleep and before starting to align everything in
the room, he was to immerse his hands in the honey and keep
them smeared for twenty minutes, during which he was free

---

*This intervention follows Haley's (1984) guidelines for the formulation of thera-
peutic ordeals.

to touch and align whatever he wanted. After twenty minutes, he was to wash his hands and ask himself whether he was ready to go to sleep. If not ready, he was to repeat the procedure until he felt sure he was going to sleep.

A week later, Solly reported on his response to the ordeal. He had used the honey pot twice and the compulsion had vanished. When asked whether he had experienced much anxiety, Solly replied, smiling, that it had all been exquisitely pleasurable. He would immerse his hands in honey, close his eyes, and imagine himself in his mother's impeccably clean and orderly house, smearing things with honey and putting them in the most improbable places.

Therapy then proceeded to the dating problem. Solly brought two girls to his mother's and enjoyed predicting in advance all the criticisms she would make. Other issues of autonomous choice surfaced and were handled in a similar spirit. A year later, when therapy was concluded, Solly was still symptom free and felt he had made a big step in learning what he wanted and trying to achieve it.

The initial message and the ordeal that followed it exemplify a variety of ways to enhance the impact of interventions. The message gathered power by unifying the therapeutic issues that had been previously disjointed. Furthermore, by contraposing pairs of themes (the gods and the mother, the dependence and the compulsion), the message capitalized on our memory for polarities. The ordeal achieved impact by arousing curiosity, exacting commitment, and administering a humorous shock. The two aspects of impact, drama and work, figured in equal parts in this intervention.

Case 6: A Deprived Child

A very worried couple asked for help with their four-year-old daughter, Ruhama, who never spoke a word or emitted a sound in kindergarten. At home, in contrast, Ruhama terrorized her parents, as well as her elder brother and sister, with a never-ending stream of peremptory commands and abusive epithets screamed with almost superhuman intensity. She also developed compulsive rituals at home, such as adjusting the position of her chair again and again whenever she sat at the table (she always ate alone), and dictating to her mother the exact words she had to say when putting her to sleep, waking her up, or sending her to kindergarten. The parents had taken her to a neurologist, who performed a thorough examination including a complete battery of tests. Although there were no pathological findings, they still felt sure that something was deeply wrong with Ruhama.

The mother, in particular, felt completely at Ruhama's mercy. She had lost all semblance of authority after having for a few days left Ruhama, along with her brother and sister, in the care of an aunt, on the occasion of a trip abroad with her husband. Ruhama never stopped whining and clung to her ten-year-old sister for the whole duration of the trip. Once the parents returned, she remained moody for weeks. The mother felt terribly guilty, and from then on she spent all her time at home caring for Ruhama, giving in to her every whim, and trying to undo the damage she had done by expressing love even when all she felt was anger and despair.

The therapist brought the case to the consultation group in order to check whether the depth of the disturbance contraindicated clear educational measures, calling instead for a long-term, cautious approach. Ruhama's behavior with the therapist (she agreed to communicate by drawings and games) suggested, however, that from behind the virago, a lively, curious, and sociable child was peeping out. In spite of this impression, the suspicion of deep pathology still proved quite paralyzing to the therapist, as it had to the parents. To compete with these disabling apprehensions, the intervention had to be couched in very strong terms:

In my examination of your daughter I found no pathological signs, but I did find deep deprivation. Ruhama suffers from deprivation in two major areas, and the deprivation deepens as she grows. Unless the deprivation is remedied, Ruhama will not develop as she should. I will now describe to you the two areas, and I know you will both be very surprised. Here it is: Ruhama suffers from parental deprivation. There is no parental presence in her life. She has a maternal deprivation; she lacks a mother. You, mother, will surely say, "But I am with her all the time, and all my life is hers!" That's precisely the point. Ruhama has a servant, a chambermaid, a slave, but no mother. You have suppressed your presence and your personality before her. You are her wishes, her needs, her voice. Not her mother.

What does it mean to have a mother? It means having another person present, with her own needs, personality, and wants. Without such presence the child feels deserted, for there is nobody there. Your self-suppression traumatizes Ruhama just as you think that she was traumatized when you left her with her aunt: you leave her motherless.

Ruhama screams at you and treats you as a doormat, but you hug her in return. You are not there as a person: this is maternal deprivation. But you, father, deprive her of your presence too. When you try to do something different, as soon as Ruhama starts crying and mother comes in with consolation, you draw aside. So she has no father either. When a child kicks a parent, the parent gets angry and the child must know this, otherwise the child doesn't feel the parent. Ruhama may feel that she has a machine that works according to certain rules, but no parents. When she does all these things to you, you are angry. But how is this anger expressed? Not openly, but in the form *of destructive worries, such as thinking that Ruhama is crazy, neurologically impaired, or whatever. So long as you continue to suppress your just parental anger, you will go on thinking that something is wrong with her head. And so long as you think so, you will not be able to provide her with a real parental presence, and will thus continue to traumatize her. To remedy Ruhama's deprivation, you must get yourselves back as persons and as parents. You both have to find your voices again.*

The second deprivation is linked to the first. Ruhama suffers from a boundary deprivation. She needs external boundaries in order to grow, just as much as she needs love, food and play. In her want of external boundaries, she invents absurd rules to fill their empty place, such as moving the chair again and again until it is perfectly aligned.

Why does Ruhama scream at home and remain mute at kindergarten? At home she screams because it makes her the omnipotent sovereign. At kindergarten it is not even worth trying, for she can, at best, be one among many. The more she screams her way at home, the less will it be worth her while to speak at kindergarten. When she grows less powerful at home, it may be worth her while to become a citizen in her second country, kindergarten.

After the initial shock, a discussion followed on how to implement the new ideas. The parents chose to start with the screaming. With the therapist's approval, they decided to wear earplugs whenever Ruhama raised her voice. This symbolic gesture signaled their readiness to fight, and Ruhama started to respond. In a few weeks she had stopped screaming and behaving compulsively, and had begun talking with children at kindergarten. After three months, the parents felt quite effective at home, were happy with Ruhama's much improved social life (for a while she had reacted to the parents' putting on earplugs by talking through the window to children in the street), and were only dissatisfied with the fact that Ruhama still did not talk to the grown-ups at kindergarten. There was no longer mention of neurological or mental impairment.

In terms of impact factors, this intervention began by creating suspense, developing an atmosphere of urgency, and striking a completely unexpected note. The talk of "deprivation" resonated with the parental feeling that something was deeply wrong, so that the message did not sound irrelevant as the neurologist's report had. The choice of earplugs for containing Ruhama's vocal bullying was a physical reminder, at the home scene, of the critical message. The intervention was thus brought into direct contact with the problem, impinging on a very critical spot (the parents' ears).

By means such as these impact is promoted. Impact, however, says nothing about whether the message is right or wrong. In fact, a very bad message might be conveyed with high impact, making its damage deeper and more lasting. We have all occasionally felt the temptation to "resolve" an agonizing impasse by sending the patient home packed with a load of impactful psychological imprecations. Impasse resolution is surely not a matter of impact alone. It requires, as detailed in the following chapters, a judicious analysis and dismantlement of the narratives, strategies, and interactions that perpetuate therapeutic deadlock.

3

NARRATIVE

RECONSTRUCTION

THE VIEW OF THERAPY AS A process of narrative reconstruction has lately grown highly influential. It has been
embraced by psychoanalysts (Schafer, 1982; Spence, 1982,
1987), family therapists (Boscolo, Cecchin, Hoffman, & Penn,
1987; White & Epston, 1990), cognitive therapists (Russel &
van den Broek, 1992), followers of integrative or eclectic
approaches (Omer & Strenger, 1992), and brief psychotherapists (Gustafson, 1992; Strupp & Binder, 1984), as well as by
well-known theoreticians who are not identified with any
particular therapeutic orientation (Bruner, 1986; Gergen &
Gergen, 1986; Sarbin, 1986). This wide appeal stems from a
variety of sources, including: (1) the demise of the schools
and of the assumption that therapy uncovers the unique
hidden truth of past events (Omer & London, 1988); (2) the
growing belief, in all fields of psychology, that the mind
construes the perceived world, determining how we experi-

ence it; and (3) the rise of hermeneutics as a general perspective on knowledge, culture, and the growth of personality (Messer, Sass, & Woolfolk, 1988). Behind all these, however, may well lie the high regard of psychotherapists for the well-wrought case-story. Great therapists are great storytellers: good therapy might turn out to be good storying.

The implications of this narrative perspective have as yet only been sketched. In the traditional view, the business of therapy was to diagnose mental illness and remove its causes. This entailed a thorough knowledge of psychopathological categories and their etiology, and of unique treatment tools for unearthing and undoing what the past did. Only one cure could be real: the one that reversed the process of pathogenesis. Approaches such as the behavioral, which opposed this medical terminology, shared its realistic and deterministic assumptions: behavioral problems stemmed from objective environmental causes which treatment had to remove. Again, there could be only one real treatment: the one that fit the real cause. False treatments could achieve only apparent cures that left the patient even worse off, or chance cures that stumbled erratically and unwittingly upon the real cause. The assumptions of the narrative model are totally different. Problems result from the way we construe our lives, play our roles and interact with the construals of others. The process of therapy consists in trying out alternative construals, none of which is uniquely right. Any problem may thus be solved in many ways, each giving rise to new experiences and to new problems.

This view might look like old wine in new bottles: "cure" becomes "renarration" but therapy remains the same. Not so, however. The new assumptions are proving subversive of practice as well as of theory, giving rise to new treatment concepts and tools. For example, a typology of flawed narratives is emerging, fulfilling some of the roles that, but recently, belonged exclusively to psychopathology.

A TYPOLOGY OF FLAWED NARRATIVES

Patchy and Chaotic Narratives

The patchy or chaotic narrative is characterized by gaps and leaps: crucial episodes are missing, stages skipped, and causal links omitted. Spence (1983) argued that the core of identity, the sense of self, is a *continuous* narrative thread that gives unity and meaning to life:

> Talk to patients in a fugue state ... with Korsakoff's syndrome or Alzheimer's disease, and you will sense the terror that lies behind not knowing who you are, what happened yesterday and what will happen tomorrow. Part of my sense of self depends on my being able to go backward and forward in time and weave a story about who I am, how I got that way, and where I am going, a story that is continuously nourishing and self-sustaining. Take that away from me and I am significantly less. In the final analysis, living only for the moment, I am not a person at all. (p. 458)

In psychotherapy, we usually meet with more selective gaps and leaps than in Alzheimer's or Korsakoff's disease. Still, the sense of self may be badly truncated or skewed. People's lives can be tossed by incongruent stories that lack a central theme, a sense of continuous agency, or an orderly line of development. Others enact a story with one repetitive characteristic gap, such as the consistent omission of their own acts, the desires of others, or the emotional side of events. For still others the story's sketchiness is due to a single-minded focus on one kind of experience to the exclusion of all else: they tell their lives, for instance, as a long series of betrayals or failures.

On the surface, there is little novelty here. Therapy has always concerned itself with memory gaps. Traditionally, however, the stress fell on the missing experiences; today, it falls on the need for a smooth narrative. Thus, there is no longer a specific repressed memory that has to be unearthed, failing which, the patient will not heal. Links are what is needed and continuity is valued *per se*.

The Closed Narrative

Closed narratives are so framed as to eliminate positive options and lead inexorably to a bad ending. Their power stems from our being so immersed in them that they become the medium through which we perceive: problem-free areas go undetected. Gustafson (1992) described three of their commonest types: the *subservience story* of people who cooperate with being put down while building up resentment; the *delay story* of those that put off living so as to avoid painful feelings; and the *overpowering story* of the domineering who engender hostility all around. These stories seem unescapable because what is viewed as the only alternative (*the shadow story*) turns out to be a loop that reintroduces the main line. Thus, subservient characters may erupt in punitive raids against their oppressors, but get so scared that they must beg reacceptance as bona fide victims; delayers occasionally approach their out-of-bounds life-stream, but find that the current has meanwhile grown much too strong; and bullies may try to give up bossing only to find themselves about to be trampled by their vengeful victims. The attempted release thus becomes just another turn of the screw.

Gustafson's concept of *the shadow story* characterizes a whole family of closed narratives. For instance, the character in a story of trauma, for whom before the trauma all was good and after which all is bad, may opt for release through pleasurable activities (the shadow story); as these fail to yield any pleasure comparable to that of pre-trauma days, the closed narrative becomes even more tightly closed.

Meaningless Narratives

Want of meaning in life stories may manifest itself as a sense of absurdity, triviality, or inauthenticity, to mention but a few of its many forms: a trivial story is one that is experienced as inane; an inauthentic story figures a character without an inner voice; and an absurd story, a life at odds with the world. These experiences have supplied the argument for innumerable books and films. Emptiness proves to be a very rich subject.

We may ask again, "What is new here?" Psychotherapy has always searched for the hidden meaning of events. The difference lies in the assumptions. In the schools' era, the search was for the *one true meaning* (Strenger & Omer, 1992), be it the hidden historical cause, the unique purpose of an individual's existence, or the real emotion behind appearances. In the pluralist era, meaning is no longer *there* to be found, but is continuously construed, tried on and modified. As our life changes, we reinterpret events, and as we reinterpret them, life changes. Consider a hedonist: his life is full or empty according to the quantum of pleasure yielded by events. Suddenly, he undergoes religious conversion: the whole of past and future life reverses its value and meaning. From a unitary religious perspective, the hedonist has found the true meaning of life; from a pluralist one, a new life narrative has been created, with new landscapes, heroes, and adventures.

PSYCHO-EDITORIAL PRINCIPLES

A typology of flawed stories implies a set of psycho-editorial principles for their repair. For example, "establish continuities" (Omer & Alon, in press), "search for missing links," and "bring about thematic unity" (Strupp & Binder, 1984) are possible rules for dealing with chaotic and patchy stories; "challenge the story's assumptions," "focus on unique outcomes"* (White & Epston, 1990) are prescriptions for addressing closed narratives; "increase emotional involvement," "search for hidden

---

*In White and Epston's terminology, *unique outcomes* are events that do not fit with the closed narrative's expected course. They are thus the potential seeds of the new narrative.

meanings," "strive for a sense of purpose," "find a moral for the story," "increase the sense of personal agency" are all possible avenues to the meaningless narrative. From a pluralist perspective, any rule may prove helpful in some cases but damaging in others. Thus, finding a hidden meaning makes problems understandable, but perhaps also inescapable ("With a past like mine how could I behave otherwise?"); developing a sense of purpose helps overcome despair, but may also engender rigidity ("How can I enjoy myself when I should serve as a living memorial to the Holocaust?"); and endowing the story with a moral may help to avoid mistakes, but may also become a tool to badger oneself and others with ("I was cheated once and will never trust anyone again"). In the pluralist era, no principle can aspire to absolute status, and no set of principles to comprehensiveness. The following principles, besides reflecting my preferences, have proved particularly valuable in the development of critical interventions.

Gain a Narrative Foothold

Personal narratives are not encapsulated intrapsychic constructs, which dwell in splendid isolation within the mind. On the contrary, they are born and fed by dialogue and exist only as part of a net of other characters and storymakers, such as one's family, friends, and colleagues. People who come to therapy are usually those whose self-narratives fail to profit from this give-and-take with a narrating network. Their interactions with others seem only to bind them ever more tightly to their self-limiting descriptions. Consider a patient who, following a personal misfortune, develops the complaints and disabilities often labeled "post-traumatic stress disorder." Such a patient usually views him or herself as a victim of circumstances. This view is strengthened by the psychiatric diagnosis, which confirms that the patient's suffering is a disease resulting from trauma. People close to the patient usually accept this description and participate in its enactment. Thus, family members start to discharge some of the roles that the patient feels unable to perform, initially as temporary arrangements but eventually as permanent ones.

As the "illness-incapacity" story crystallizes, some try to contest it, viewing the patient as one who exploits the status of a victim in order to gain benefits. People in official positions, for instance, may challenge the patient's psychiatric status, arguing that the problem is chiefly motivational and that it will only be aggravated by further concessions. This oppositional stance does little to mollify the patient's view of the problem. On the contrary, any change away from the "illness-incapacity" version would now be perceived by the patient as tantamount to a confession of guilt and a proclamation of the persecutors' victory. Thus, both those who share and those who contest the patient's story end up making it ever more rigid and entrenched.

Similarly, a therapy that placed itself at any of these poles would hardly be able to help. Identifying with or contesting the patient's narrative would only contribute to its maintenance. The therapist should begin from the patient's premises and follow the drift of the patient's story, but should then help him or her to move away from it.* For instance, the therapist might start by lending a clear voice to the patient's perspective and feelings, thereby gaining a foothold in the narrative network. This echoing of the patient's experience should not be expressed as reflecting the therapist's own position but as an empathic understanding. The therapeutic leverage rests upon this foothold, deriving its power of influence from its initial resonance with the self-narrative.

---

*This principle has been independently described under a variety of names by proponents of different therapeutic approaches. For instance, "joining" (Minuchin, 1974), "pacing and leading" (Haley, 1973), and "modality matching" (Lazarus, 1981).

Most of the critical messages in this book follow this pattern of gaining a foothold within the patient's self-narrative before moving away from it. In case 1 ("A trap of competitiveness"), for instance, the intervention begins by positively echoing the patient's need for challenges; in case 2 ("Bondage and devotion"), by highlighting the patient's unique work of love and loyalty; in case 3 ("A problem of self-esteem"), by resonating with the patient's sense of a basic flaw. Practically all the other cases would provide cogent illustrations.

Detrivialize Suffering

Psychotherapists often get a bad name for ascribing too much meaning to trivial events. Thus, a patient who arrives early to a session is anxious, one who arrives late is acting out, and one who arrives on time is obsessive. There is wisdom in this caricature, for it shows the common mistake of ascribing meaning in a way that makes sense to the therapist but not to the patient. However, when events are invested with a personal significance and imbued with sense out of the patient's own language and values, then there is no such thing as "too much meaning." This is especially true when pain and suffering are concerned.

Pain is bad enough, but it can be so much worse if it is sensed as paltry. Pointing out to people that their situation is not too serious, that others have suffered more, that the pain is fruitless and best forgotten, or that it is irrational and therefore unnecessary, robs the sufferer of the consolation of experiencing pain as momentous, special, and honorable. Such "encouragement" leaves the sufferer more alone, and often with a sense of having been slighted and misunderstood.

In the following case, the therapist's attempt to minimize pain unwittingly fed the very sense of meaninglessness from which the patient suffered. The critical intervention aimed to reverse this situation by showing that the apparently trivial causes of the patient's pain drew their power from the weighty issues on which they were grafted.

Case 7: Two Kinds of Suffering

Mrs. Rose was a 79-year-old woman who complained of a big change in her life that made her suspect she was going crazy. It all began with the donation of $10,000 to a television preacher, which she had made under pressure, two years previously. The preacher had applied to her for a contribution and pressed home his request by endless phone calls and visits. She gave him $5,000, but this only doubled the pressure. She ended up by reaching an agreement with him, whereby she would give him another $5,000 if he promised to leave her alone. He kept the promise.

Mrs. Rose soon began worrying that she had given money to the wrong cause. She would spend hours every day examining all possible applicants for philanthropic aid. She decided to limit herself to $30 in donations a day, but then blamed herself for not being a "cheerful giver."

Three months later someone crashed into her car's bumper in a parking lot. She had the bumper fixed, but remained obsessed with the idea that it was badly aligned. She felt angry for having been cheated, but blamed herself for being puny. She had heard about people with multiple personality and thought she might have it, for she seemed so different from what she had always been. She also obsessed endlessly about her affairs and papers, fearing that she might die suddenly, leaving a mess for her children to sort out.

In spite of these troubles and almost constant feelings of depression, Mrs. Rose was very active: she socialized, had a positive relationship with her two sons who visited her often, was busy with the church, and worked as a volunteer in a philanthropic organization. A big change, however, had taken place in her social life: one of her closest woman friends had died a couple of years before. Mrs. Rose missed her badly, but was sure that she was in heaven. As for herself, she was not quite sure about her place in heaven.

During the first two months of therapy, Mrs. Rose told and retold the stories of the donation and the bumper, and repeatedly expressed her wish "to get to the bottom of her problem." She also kept asking the therapist if she was paranoid, schizophrenic, or had multiple personality. The therapist reassured her that she suffered from none of those diseases. Mrs. Rose, however, was not satisfied. She included a special request to God in her daily prayers to the effect that He might help her therapist "to get to the bottom of her problem." The therapist tried to encourage Mrs. Rose and reduce her irrational worries, but Mrs. Rose only felt that the therapist still did not really understand her problem.

An attempt to explore Mrs. Rose's past also proved singularly unhelpful. She would reminisce nostalgically about her childhood, but gave no details whatsoever about her family. Neither had she anything to say about her forty years of marriage, except for complaining vaguely that she had not been a good wife and mother. Whenever the therapist tried to clarify these issues, Mrs. Rose would veer back to the donation, the bumper, and the craziness. To her mind, time spent talking of other matters was time wasted.

The therapist made a diagnosis of obsessive-compulsive disorder. The obsessions, interpreted by the therapist as due to irrational guilt feelings, were the dominant feature. This conceptualization of the problem and the cognitive supportive strategy chosen by the therapist to deal with it led to a complementary interaction, for encouragment and rational explanation made Mrs. Rose feel misunderstood. Telling Mrs. Rose that her mistakes were no crimes, that she did not suffer from paranoia or multiple personality, or that her sons loved and respected her (as the therapist had ascertained by talking to them on the phone), made her sufferings seem even more absurd and turned her life into a sequence of trivial despairs. Treatment was making the problem worse. The following message was designed, in the course of a consultation, to open the way for a different dialogue:

I have come to realize that your feeling that something is fundamentally wrong with you is justified. In the past I tried, mistakenly, to prescribe for you mental aspirins, which only made you feel misunderstood. I can see now that your sense of something wrong within you is not irrational, but is deeply linked to your religiosity. Maybe a person without your religious feelings would feel comfortable with the things you did in your life, but this is not to the point, because what matters is what you feel.

What is the source of this sense that something is amiss? Perhaps some of it may have to do with things that must remain a secret between you and God. Some of it may be hazy, even to you, manifesting itself just as a vague, oppressive discomfort, such as your sense that you were not a good wife and mother. Whatever the reason, however, you feel that your spiritual affairs are not in order. You are sure that your friend who passed away is in heaven, but you are not at all sure about what lies in store for you. You are almost eighty, and you don't feel ready to face your Maker.

For the last two years, something has seemed continually wrong, out of place and out of joint, but you cannot pinpoint what it is or how it can be righted. You feel unable to atone and to make reparation all by yourself. People with a religious sense always feel that they cannot do good all by themselves, and that they need divine guidance and grace to steady their efforts. So, you pray to God to help you and to help me help you.

Your suffering comes from events that, to your mind, are trivial and petty. For instance, you feel that you fret too much about giving and are not a cheerful giver. You feel selfish and puny in being so punctillious about your bumper. This endless worrying about seemingly small matters makes you think that you may be mad. All of this suffering seems meaningless and absurd to you, but I think that it has a deep meaning. I don't think that your worries about the bumper are vain. I think they carry a message: you feel that something is misaligned. And truly, although you seem to worry about the bumper, the suffering comes from feeling that your life is misaligned. This suffering is of the greatest importance: it is part of your spiritual stocktaking, of your getting ready to face your Maker. You suffer daily that your affairs are not in good order. Again, I believe there is no quibbling in that. You worry about disorder in worldly affairs, but your suffering comes from disorder in your spiritual affairs. You said that one of the reasons you felt bad about your donation was that it deprived your sons of something that was rightfully theirs. Again, the real pain comes from a deep source: you feel that you were not a good mother.

I want to help you to find the seriousness behind the trivia, to look for the meaning and the message in the suffering. We are imperfect and cannot order our spiritual affairs fully in this life. In realizing my mistake, however, I feel that I have learnt something of value. You have helped me to this, and I want to help you in turn. Working together, with hope, we may find some of the true meaning behind your worries. Sometimes we will fail and the suffering may still seem trivial and unjustified. Even then, however, you will be making reparation, for you know that no suffering is meaningless in the eyes of God.

A follow-up with the therapist was carried out by mail.* The message was never delivered. The consultation had failed to assess the therapist's difficulty in changing her previous stance. A visit of Mrs. Rose's sons on the occasion of her eightieth birthday provided the therapist with an opportunity of playing her usual supportive role more effectively. She held a meeting with all three, in which the sons expressed their love and admiration for their mother. In a further session with the sons alone, a plan was developed for a birthday party in which they would reminisce positively and in detail about the past. The visit and the party made a deep impression. The obsession and the depression cleared up completely. A year later, however, the symptoms reappeared and Mrs. Rose was assigned to a new therapist (the former one had left the clinic), to whom she told all over again the unfortunate tale of her donation, her bumper and her craziness.

Invest the Patient as a Hero

Patients should be heroes, not bystanders, in their life stories. Focusing on the narrative's protagonist, this principle complements the former one ("detrivialize suffering"), which focused on the narrative's events. Together, they aim at changing the experience of life as a spate of occurrences irrelevant and indifferent to one's wishes, values, and acts.

Heroes are not necessarily triumphant, but even the tale of a tragic hero is preferable to that of an extra. Faced with inescapable fate, the tragic hero expresses feelings and values that are deeply human. The life of an extra expresses nothing. It floats and sinks with the current, leaving not even the record of a voice. The role of the hero contrasts also with the usual role of the victim. Heroes, as much as victims, can be broken, but the hero's life remains significant even in defeat.

---

*This consultation took place during a brief visit of mine to the U.S.

It is not the daring stance and the grim countenance that make the hero. The therapeutic investment of one is a complex act of reconstruction, whereby therapist helps patient to transform blind events into the stages of a quest, charging obstacles with significance and imbuing personal relationships with quasi-legendary qualities. Thus, a routine difficulty is turned into a test, an unfamiliar event into a baptism, a sign of trust into a blessing, a label into a malignant prophecy, and family members into brothers-in-arms, conspirators and witches.* The terms of the reconstruction must fit the patient. It would be silly, for instance, to retell the story of a woman who is fighting for independence and equality as one of a damsel in distress or to redescribe an adolescent who perceives himself as weak but cunning as an armored knight. In our skeptical age, the gap between a redeeming and a ridiculous tale is exceedingly narrow, and therapists should proceed with care.

Case 8: Drabness or Chivalry

Herman was a 35-year-old accountant who postponed everything. In spite of his intelligence, he was a professional failure. He contracted debts and lived in the expectation of financial disaster, investing all his energy in last ditch efforts to ward off the incipient cataclysm by means of tricky combinations that gained him a few days' breathing space at a time. He would beam with excitement when telling the therapist about his brilliant escapes. The therapist came to believe that Herman was "addicted to the thrill of imminent catastrophe."

---

*One does not need to speak of gods and monsters to turn therapy into a fabled odyssey. The world of psychotherapy is rich in quasi-mythical terms, such as the trauma of birth, the oedipal triangle, the primeval oceanic feeling, the language of dreams, the family scapegoat, the family conspiracy, ego, id and superego, the archetypes of the collective unconscious, the true and the false self, the self-actualizing journey, the inner voice, and the outer mask. Even the deliberately anti-mythical terminology of behavioral and the cognitive approaches provides the therapist with good mythical substitutes such as the titanic battle between rational and irrational thoughts, and the ordeal of implosion.

For the last five years he had been involved in a relationship with a married woman whom he described as perfection incarnate. He dreamed about her, composed music celebrating her, and lived for her alone. Because of her, he felt he must get rich. She loved him, but she was "a lady of high standards" and he could only win her from her husband by offering her a glamorous life. In his eagerness to make a huge profit he had, of late, committed a felony: he had laid hands on money put in his trust by a friend of his beloved's, risked it, and lost it. He lived in fear that, once discovered, this would shatter his image in the eyes of his beloved. He searched for ways to replace the sum, but his other debts sucked in whatever money he succeeded in scraping off.

The therapist had tried to deal with Herman's procrastination by cognitive-behavioral techniques. Herman would make some progress, tackling some long avoided cases and ordering his chaotic schedule a bit, but soon a new threat would wipe out all gains as Herman engaged in a frantic search for escape. After four months of Sisyphean work, the therapist reached the conclusion that Herman was no partner for cognitive-behavior therapy, and that a confrontation with the unrealistic nature of his fantasies and, possibly, with the need for a career change should be attempted. However, even mentioning to Herman that his goal (money and the lady) seemed impracticable made him furious. He was confident that he would achieve a breakthrough, either through his brilliance as an accountant or by a financial coup.

In Herman's eyes, his life was a string of ill-starred episodes interspersed with occasional inebriating moments of ineffable bliss. He still believed, however, that success and happiness lay just around the corner, depending only on the right blend of good luck and good therapy. In the therapist's eyes, the ups and downs of Herman's life were inextricably linked to his romanticism. There was no way of making him more effective that would not also make him less romantic. Herman could either be an accountant or a dreamer. The attempt to be both was preposterous.

Herman and the therapist held mutually exclusive narratives. The following message was thereupon devised to create a narrative that could be shared by both, while also releasing the therapist from his ungrateful role as purveyor of sober techniques to a tempest-loving client. The question was whether the therapeutic alliance could survive this change. Some members in the consultation group believed that the message would be a prologue to termination.

I have had second thoughts lately about what would happen if you became a good, efficient accountant. You would lead a calmer life, the office would function, and things would seem normal. But I think they would also become very drab. You are a romantic figure, spurred by love, inspired by music and surrounded by danger. There can be few things so alien to your nature as an orderly office.

You may think it strange, but many people dream of a life like yours. It is a succession of adventures, vital threats, and narrow escapes. You fight danger daily and survive by cunning. You never know how the day will end. You are a modern knight-errant. You don't seek adventure for the fun of it, but to be worthy of the woman you love. Being with her is the realization of all your earthly wishes, but you must achieve total victory for this total bliss. If your beloved were to come to you before the time were ripe, it would mean disaster. So you must go on, fighting for your life and love, making the most of your brains and luck.

How can a man who lives as you live find himself at a different stage of life? What does perilous knighthood turn into? Though there seems to be no way out in the immediate future, in another few years you may become mellower, the ups and downs may grow less steep, you may feel tired. Or, who knows, maybe all will end in a big bang.

You wanted me to help you to bring some order into your office, some plan into your weekly schedule. I failed in this task. I am not a good Sancho Panza. Were I to continue in this line, failing again and again, I might think of you too as a failure. Maybe it would be better for me to sit with you, listen to your adventures and to your tales of love, and help you to see the whole story in large. Instead of focusing on what you should do tomorrow at the office, we might look at the larger meaning of your quest, retrace the course of your wanderings and ponder on the meaning of what met you along the way. This is not a utilitarian dialogue. It will not solve any problems at short notice, but it may lead to other changes. You might learn to see yourself differently, not so much as a victim of circumstance, but as a hero. Truly, you might find out that you are a bungling hero or a quixotic hero, but nonetheless the hero of your life.

Herman reacted by a surprising move. He took the heroic plunge of telling his beloved about his financial troubles and about what he had done with her friend's money. She responded lovingly and supportively. Herman took warmly to the new view of himself as a romantic hero and for a while it seemed as if therapy had embarked on a new course. The new dialogue, however, did not survive for long. A few more sessions led to a friendly and mutually appreciative (but premature) termination. The critical intervention had failed to inspire a normal therapy. The therapist felt that Herman would soon look for another therapist to bring some order into his life. He did.

Create Options by a New Character

The addition of a new character to expand narrative options is a well-trodden path of narrative transformation. The new char-

acter comments upon and thereby modifies the interaction between the other ones. Alternatively, the new character serves
as an unbalancing factor, casting its weight upon one of the
sides or pulling it in a different direction.

Psychotherapy often gets stuck in a narrative that perpetu-
ates stalemated dualities such as: husband/wife, parents/chil-
dren, patient/"others," and supporters/persecutors. Ideally, the
therapist should maintain the neutral stance of interpreter or
commentator, instilling movement into the hardened polarities. All too often, however, the therapist also gets involved in
an oppositional framework (with the patient or with other major characters in the patient's surroundings), further entrench-
ing the balance of power and deepening the impasse it set out
to resolve.

In the history of psychotherapy, the solution to a two-party
stalemate often came from the addition of a third party, either
on the therapeutic stage itself (the co-therapist or a new family
member) or behind stage (the supervisor or the team behind
the one-way mirror). The third party, however, does not have
to be present in the flesh in order to perform its unbalancing
function. A new character, who is depicted as the patient's
friend or foe, may be added to the therapeutic narrative. This
virtual presence may carry enough weight to tip the scales, as
shown in the following case.

Case 9: In the Footsteps of the Mother-in-Law

Judith had been divorced from John for two years when she
became obsessed by an urge to go back to him, in spite of the
promptings of her better judgment and of practically everyone
who cared for her. They had been married for 25 years and
had three children (aged 8, 16, and 20). John was a businessman
whose shady dealings had suddenly burst into the open, forcing
him to leave Israel for the U.S. Just before he left she succeeded in getting a last-minute divorce from him with the help

of a generous financial settlement. Her father played a crucial role by agreeing to assume some of John's most risky debts.

In the beginning John seldom wrote or phoned. Judith managed well without him, finishing with distinction a long-drawn-out Ph.D. in archaeology, which brought her an academic position, and developing an active social life. Neither she nor the children missed him. Suddenly, however, John began to shower her with effusive love letters and hold lengthy conversations with her on the phone, blaming himself for all that had happened and promising her a new life. In his talks, he alluded to another woman who was waiting in the wings if Judith failed him. His financial situation was still precarious. Lacking a green card, he was making a living, once again, by somewhat shadowy means. These reminders of John's tendencies might have chilled Judith's ardor, but the mention of the other woman threw her into a jealous frenzy. John fawned, begged and lied. In his zeal, he blundered and overplayed his card, for instance, by telling Judith that he had talked of marriage to the other woman. When Judith slammed down the phone, he called again and excoriated himself for all his present and past sins, baffling her thoroughly. He even convinced the other woman (or was it all a put-up?) to phone Judith and tell her that she (Judith) was the one whom John really loved! Judith was so confused that she ended up buying a ticket to the U.S. so as to check her feelings for him on the spot. She came to therapy because her father, friends, and elder children begged her not to make the trip, telling her that nothing but trouble would come from John. All reminded her of how miserable her marriage had been, how John had never given her affection, support or respect, how he had hampered her academic development and lied to her no end.

Judith also had bitter memories of her mother-in-law, who adored John and had warned Judith before the marriage to leave him alone, for he deserved a better match. After the marriage, she had treated Judith like a doormat, sometimes going to the extreme of serving a meal for John alone when both came to a visit. Whenever Judith tried to raise the issue with John, he would tell her not to pay attention, for everybody knew his mom was crazy. When they divorced, the mother-in-law threw a party and declared that now that John had rid himself of Judith he would soon achieve the success and recognition he deserved. She became active in arranging a proper match for him abroad, but died before achieving this goal. Without the mother-in-law, Judith thought that she might, for the first time, get really close to John.

The therapist asked Judith whether she had any hopes that John would change. Judith replied that she now understood how she had also been to blame: she had been inhibited in sex, had shown little warmth to John or the children, and had always been critical and pessimistic. Even now, when she thought of John, bad things came to her mind, but she believed that for once she should trust her warmer feelings. She had never really loved; maybe this was her chance. It seemed that the more people tried to make her see reason, the more emotional she became. The therapist felt that any attempt to describe John in an objective light would turn the therapeutic dialogue into a similar tug-of-war. On the other hand, she felt that by withholding her professional opinion about John, she might be doing Judith even greater damage. This dilemma brought the therapist to a consultation, two weeks before Judith's scheduled trip.

No one in the group had any doubts about John. Group members found themselves competing for who could describe his personality disorder in the worst professional terms. The direst psychopathological labels, however, would not make Judith budge an inch. On the contrary, she might cling to her newborn feelings all the more for their being crossed. The charge of absurdness is oil to the romantic flame. As long as Judith could construe her story as one of opposition between her warm feelings and the cold reason of others', no movement would ensue. The following text was devised to break this symmetric deadlock and contaminate Judith's romantic perspective with the aid of a third character.

For the first time in your life you are experiencing a surge of romantic emotions. You feel that by obeying cold reason you may waste your chance for a fuller life. People tell you that meeting with John is an awful mistake, but for you it is the call of duty: you can't turn a deaf ear to your feelings.

The death of your mother-in-law makes a huge change. Whatever you may think of her, she surely loved him deeply. She knew who John was and she adored him. The world was wrong, you were to blame, but John was spotless. Her love for him was characterized by full, unconditional forgiveness. Indeed, John seems to arouse forgiveness and admiration in many people. Even this woman, whom he has ostensibly considered marrying, seems willing to forgive and help him, while he uses her for his ends. Nobody, however, could ever forgive him so absolutely as his mother did. She not only forgave him but was deaf and blind to his faults. Her absence may leave a space for you to fill.

Forgiveness seems to be growing within you. While your family and friends are sure that he is a downright crook, you cherish him in your heart. Forgiving John seems to be the way to loving him. This may be the key to your relationship. You must be willing to forgive and forget without keeping a mental account of your grievances. He will probably make trouble, for troublemaking is his nature. If, however, you are determined to follow your warm feelings to the end, you may have a chance. It may be unpleasant to think about it this way, but now that your mother-in-law is no longer there, you can follow in her footsteps into the way of forgiveness. You may be in for a bitter disappointment, but you feel that you must try. This seems now to be your duty to your feelings.

Judith did not accept the message at face value. She challenged the comparison with her mother-in-law and questioned the necessity for self-sacrifice. She decided, however, to take her youngest son with her to the U.S., as a shield against premature intimacy with John. As a further precaution, she phoned the therapist every other day during her stay abroad. She came back in a much cooler frame of mind. The obsessions cleared and the telephone romance stopped. She now thought that her major problem was that, except for John, she had had no experience with men. She wanted to change this. Normal therapy was resumed in this direction. However, for as long as an alternative failed to materialize, John's presence remained in the background as a hazy possibility.

CONCLUSION: THE QUASI-LITERARY SIDE OF PSYCHOTHERAPY

The image of psychotherapy as reflected in these cases seems a far cry from its accepted view as a scientifically based medicine of the mind. There is little here to remind us of the scientist or the physician. Indeed, in recent years, psychotherapy has been compared to other model disciplines, such as rhetorics (Frank, 1987) and hermeneutics (Frank, 1987; Messer, Sass, & Woolfolk, 1988). Therapists, however, can derive little guidance from these models, as a modern-day therapist hardly has a chance to meet with a rhetorician or hermeneuticist. A closer professional affinity, however, obtains with the person-of-letters. The shared features between the psychotherapeutic and the literary crafts have often been adumbrated, but hardly ever specified. Let us review some of them.

Psychotherapy requires skill with words. Some wordings are concrete and direct, others fuzzy and noncommittal; some are

hermeneutics — The science of interpretation, esp. of The Scriptures.
interpretative, explanatory

abstract and analytical, others pictorial and evocative; some are unforgettable, others virtually unretainable; some arouse indignation, others easy acceptance.

Therapy requires dramatic skill: a crescendo of arousal, for instance, may be right for a session that opened calmly or apathetically, but one that began in a storm might best be steered into a gradual quieting.

The form and atmosphere of the session, furthermore, should fit its contents. Thus, it would be quite inappropriate to convey a message of cognitive self-control by means of an abreactive surge, or to promote the centrality of feeling in a detached intellectual manner.

Characterization is also at a premium: modern practitioners, particularly when inclined to short-term psychotherapy, know how crucial it is to draw a patient's portrait early in the treatment, and how such a portrait may open up narrative options that would otherwise have remained dormant (Omer, in press).

The typology of flawed narratives and the provisional list of psycho-editorial principles presented in this chapter are also obvious counterparts of literary skills. The storyteller, no less than the therapist, must know how to steer a closed narrative in a surprising direction or how to develop narrative congruence even when depicting the vagaries of a chaotic mind.

This list of parallel skills could almost serve as a table of contents for a course in the fundamentals of a quasi-literary psychotherapy (Omer, 1993b). Thus, choice of words and of phrasing might be said to constitute the "semantics" and "syntax" of therapy; the evocative and emotional impact of words and images, its "poetics"; storylines, their flaws, and the ways of improving them its "narratology"; the skills of personal depiction its "characterology"; the buildup of therapeutic impact its "dramatics"; and issues of session structure its "theory of form." These subjects can and should be a part of a therapist's formation. Trainers and supervisors often fulfill this formative role spontaneously, when analyzing cases, discussing the framing of interpretations, planning a session's sequence and choosing appropriate images. A deeper awareness of the similarities, however, will allow us to perform the task not only intuitively, but intentionally and professionally. The quasi-literary side of psychotherapy should not be relegated to fickle inspiration. On the contrary, if well defined it could lead to a better understanding of the component skills that make psychotherapy a craft.

4

MODIFYING

INEFFECTIVE STRATEGIES

LIKE THE NARRATIVE CONCEPTION of therapy, the strategic perspective emerged within widely different therapeutic schools (Haley, 1973; Kanfer & Scheffe, 1988; Rabkin, 1977; Watzlawick, Weakland, & Fisch, 1974) and was described as a common factor that explains the way all psychotherapies work (Haley, 1990; Omer & Alon, 1989). *Narrative*, however, appeals mainly to nondirective therapists,* *strategy* to directive ones. *Narrative* offers a meeting ground for approaches on the psychodynamic, humanistic, and existential end of the therapeutic spectrum; *strategy* for those on the behavioral and problem-oriented end.

Strategies are relevant only when goals are precisely de-

---

*Even in the family therapy field, *narrative* has characterized the less directive approaches, such as White and Epston's (1990).

fined. It is preposterous, for instance, to develop a detailed strategy for achieving hazy goals like "getting in touch with the true self" or "achieving self-actualization." Although these goals may be personally meaningful, any specific strategy could be faulted as restricting their scope and closing potential avenues to their achievement. Furthermore, even if one had a plan, how could one know whether the goal was being approached? Strategies cannot be activated without feedback. In order to decide rationally on pursuing, improving, or relinquishing them, we must determine whether we are getting any closer to the goal, a determination that requires specificity. Strategies for compassing hazy goals are doomed to haziness.

Strategies are also irrelevant in the absence of constraints, such as of time, money, or logistics (for one may then simply pursue one's goals at one's own leisurely pace). An approach like psychoanalysis, for instance, is much less constrained in respect to time than one like crisis intervention. All in all, symptom- and problem-focused therapies are more constrained and their goals more specific, therefore they tend to be more strategically minded. Whenever the constraints of life make themselves felt, however, as when a patient is about to be fired, go into the army, or emigrate, strategic planning becomes paramount for any kind of therapy.

Strategic thinking in all fields deals almost invariably with the same basic issues: (1) goals and ways of achieving them, (2) obstacles, resistance and ways of negotiating them, (3) muster of alliances, and (4) mobilization of effort. In psychotherapy, a strategic lore has developed for dealing with these issues, and attempts have been made to codify typical mores and mistakes (Driscoll, 1984; Fisch, Weakland & Segal, 1982; Omer & Alon, 1989; Rabkin, 1977). These codes play in the strategic field a role similar to that played by psycho-editorial principles in the narrative field.

THE ELEMENTS OF STRATEGY

Goals

In terms of strategy, goal definition is the chief determinant of therapeutic success and failure. Goals that take into consideration the needs and values of patients make for strong alliances and deep involvement. All too often what we smugly call "resistance" or "lack of motivation" reflects no more than our rigid adherence to doctrinarian therapeutic goals and enshrined models of psychological health, with little consideration for the patient's pains and preferences. Even noble goals, such as independence, self-awareness, and flexibility, may at times turn into procrustean beds into which we try to fit unwilling patients. In its extreme forms, this professional disease is not hard to diagnose, as in the story of the Kübler-Ross (1969) follower who badgered his terminal patient for not dying according to the stages prescribed by the theory.

Even carefully shared goals, however, may prove impracticable. Every therapist has had the experience of driving hard at an accepted goal with a well motivated patient, and yet finding that the very effort seemed to block the way ever more tightly. Sometimes the goal is right and only the way is to blame. Occasionally, however, therapist and patient turn round and round, with the goal ever as tantalizingly out of reach. The resolution of such impasses requires a readiness to relinquish the goal without accusing the patient. Impasse resolution does not always mean therapeutic success. It means the resumption of a productive dialogue, sometimes on the very subject of the acceptance of failure.

Obstacles and Resistance

Although mindless obstacles may call for some strategic thinking, purposeful opposition forces it upon us, as shown by the classical strategic fields, such as war, sports, and diplomacy. Psychotherapy fits easily into this set: resistance is its daily bread. So much so that therapists sometimes turn its conquest into the chief task of therapy, leaving behind the original goals. This neglect, however, may be precisely the major factor in perpetuating noncooperation. It should be no more than a truism (but unfortunately it is not) that if therapy turns into a tangle of resistance, something is wrong with the therapy, and not just with the patient.

Impasses call on us to reassess the resistance, telling us how we may be failing the patient. They convey information about flawed goals, empathic failures, and bungled formulations. A good critical intervention should correct these failures. At its best, the critical intervention should not only include an admission of the therapist's share in the impasse but also make reparation for any shadow of blame that might have been incurred by the patient in the process.

Alliances

The therapist's primary ally is the client.* This is only a seeming truism, for therapists have a say in determining who the client should be. For example, when faced with the referral of an unwilling patient, the therapist may decide that the client is the person who made the referral.

The patient's cooperation should never be taken for granted. An initially motivated patient may tire, develop competing interests, or find other alliances more worthwhile than the one with the therapist. Impasses prompt us not only to examine the alliance with the client but also to muster additional support, for instance, with the patient's family, friends, and colleagues.

---

*The terms "client" and "patient" often denote different people. The patient is the person with the symptoms, the client is the one who is willing to work.

Even the broadest of alliances, however, may prove insuffi-
cient. Many a noble cause has perished to the tune of uncon-
solable cries from ineffective allies. To be of help, therapeutic
alliances must be made to work.

Effort

Motivation for change is often viewed as a given. "The patient
has no motivation" is probably the commonest epitaph in our
therapeutic cemeteries. Although patients undoubtedly come
to therapy with different levels of readiness for work, prolonged stagnation may sap the motivation of the most willing.
A successful critical intervention is then the one that succeeds
in remobilizing the client's flagging therapeutic energy.

To make itself felt, however, effort must not only be aroused
but also channelled and focused. Omer and Alon (1989) listed
a series of valuable strategic targets, concerning which there is
a consensus among the followers of almost any therapeutic
orientation. The chief among these are: the patient's behavioral and mental avoidances, ineffective repetitive solutions, rigid
patterns and rules, and unreflective dysfunctional behaviors.
On the positive side, change efforts are best leveled at targets
which are apt to trigger additional positive changes. One should
also guard against dissipation of therapeutic energy through un-
clear or multiple goals or through client inattention, neglect, and
forgetfulness.

In summary, then, failing strategies are usually characterized by any of the following typical errors:

1. Pursuing goals irrelevant to the patient
2. Pushing against unyielding obstacles and resistance
3. Failing to muster alliances
4. Failing to mobilize and concentrate effort

Cases 10 and 11, below, illustrate these errors and their attempted correction by means of a critical intervention. In both

cases, the four typical errors stemmed from a *therapeutic hidden agenda*. Hidden agendas are kept hidden because the therapist assumes that the patient is not ripe to share it. Their effects on the therapy are quite predictable: they engender incompatible goals, clutter the the therapeutic path with obstacles, aggravate resistance, sabotage alliances, and fritter away effort. Therapists, nevertheless, often cling most tightly to their hidden agendas, viewing their goals as synonymous with mental health itself.

The latter part of this chapter (including cases 12 and 13) deals with impasse situations characterized by conflicts of interests within the client system that lead to paralysis or destructive clashes. In these antithetical situations, advance may entail retreat, alliances waken counter-alliances, and defeat dwell at the heart of victory. To face them, strategy must itself become dialectical.

Case 10: Psychological or Physiological?

Burt, a 25-year-old student, always lost his erection before or right after penetration. His spine had been injured in an accident three years previously and he had never since achieved a proper orgasm during intercourse. Although a neurological examination had shown some sensory loss in the arms, hands, and legs, the examining physician ruled out an organic explanation for the sexual dysfunction. He pointed out to Burt that he suffered from no erectile or orgasmic dysfunction during masturbation. Sleep-plethysmography confirmed this medical judgment by revealing proper nightly erections.

When Burt first arrived in therapy, two and a half years after the accident, he did not raise the sexual problem, concentrating instead on his other difficulties with women. He felt always under scrutiny because of his physical handicap (a noticeable limp) and believed that a "normal" woman would have nothing to do with a "cripple." Therapy was a shaky affair for quite a while. He missed appointments and brought little material. Everything changed when the therapist raised the sexual issue directly. On this issue, Burt was willing to work.

Burt had had a close relationship with a girl, with good sex, for a year before the accident. After the accident, Burt decided to end the connection, for "it was no longer what it had been." Before coming to therapy, he had developed an almost purely physical affair with Joan, a woman of his age, whom he had met at the university. She had inhibitions of her own (having once been the victim of sexual assault) and preferred sex without penetration, which was very convenient for Burt. He felt no affection or respect for her, but enjoyed her deference to him, which persisted despite the most cavalier treatment on his part. He might sometimes take Joan to the movies or to a coffee shop with friends, but always made it clear that she was not his girlfriend. More typically, she would come to his place, they would chat for a few minutes and go to bed (The therapist: "How long after she came in, thirty minutes?"; Burt: "Noooooo! Six or seven.")

Burt tried to meet with women on a more equal basis, but he found that they soon lost interest ("They see that I am a cripple"). Once, after failing to perform sexually with one of his dates, he managed to convey the impression that she did not attract him physically, whereupon she stopped meeting with him. Burt, however, did not see how he contributed to his own rejection, viewing it as an objective consequence of his handicap. Only with Joan did he feel secure. Gradually, with the therapist's encouragement, he told her about his sexual problem. She was, as expected, very supportive.

The therapist offered to refer Burt to a sex therapist. Burt refused, for the sex therapist would surely tell him that his problem was psychological, which he knew it was not. The therapist felt that Burt was using the physical handicap as a screen for his interpersonal difficulties. Working on this assumption, she referred him to a second neurologist, hoping to rule out the physiological excuse. This time, a somewhat different verdict was returned: there was a slight sensory loss in the penile region but, in the doctor's opinion, not enough to justify the sexual dysfunction. The therapist had sent him to enlist support for her psychological interpretation, but Burt had found ammunition for his resistance instead!

The therapist wanted Burt to understand that his attachment to Joan was deeper than he thought. Burt agreed that the dates were pleasurable, but added that he could never respect a woman with no character, who gave herself away so cheaply. The therapist pointed that only with her did he feel really comfortable. Burt replied that he enjoyed the fact that Joan was so crazy about him, but he had no positive feelings towards her.

Burt's sexual functioning improved after he told Joan about his sexual problem. He became able to maintain an erection for a few minutes after penetration, but still failed to ejaculate. This frustrated him no end, for he believed fervently that one normal orgasm would change his whole attitude toward himself and toward women.

The therapist brought the case to consultation because she felt the therapy was going round in circles. The hypothesis was raised that Burt's only close ties (with Joan and with the therapist) rested on his nonperformance. Sexual success would lead Burt to dismiss his comfortable sexual partner and stop the therapy. One orgasm would thus put an end to both relationships. This smart explanation proved singularly unhelpful, offering no therapeutic options, except for interpreting the resistance.

Gradually, the elements in the therapist's hidden agenda were identified: Burt should acknowledge (even if only tacitly) the psychological basis of his sexual dysfunction, the central role of fear of intimacy in his life, and the deep meaning of his relationship with Joan. All these therapeutic goals were at variance with Burt's. The hidden agenda carried an implicit charge of somatization and sexism. Under such imputations, no wonder he did not cooperate. "Making progress" was almost tantamount to accepting blame. The therapist's goals were particularly unacceptable to Burt, because she had failed to respond to what he felt all along: that there was a physical problem with his penis. The following message was an attempt to exonerate Burt, clear up the hidden agenda and establish a real working alliance:

> *A week ago I brought your case for consultation with the staff. I felt I had been doing something wrong, but I didn't know what. My colleagues helped me see that I had failed to do justice to your physical problem. I wanted to believe that the problem was only psychological, for then, I thought, there would be more hope of improvement. You knew, however, that something was physically wrong. You felt that your loss of penile sensitivity was affecting your sexual performance, whereas the people who were supposed to treat you, including me, consistently minimized the importance of this factor. You felt justifiably misunderstood: we tacitly blamed you with inventing physiological excuses for what we saw as psychological difficulties.*
>
> *I was doubly wrong, for your handicap is physical, and it affects both your sexual dysfunction and your other difficulties with women. You feel blemished and unequal when facing a new date and can only expect to be exposed and rejected. To mitigate this pain, you've developed a way of behaving that gives you, at times, a sense of equality: you try to put down the woman you are dating and to slight her before you are slighted. This is what probably happened when you said to one of your dates that she didn't attract you sexually. You were hurt, but so was she.*
>
> *Your self-protective aggressive behavior serves also as*

a test. If your date passes the test and stays with you, you are no longer the underdog. Joan passed the test. You don't feel you love or appreciate her, but she stayed with you and she wants you, in spite of the way you treat her.

I didn't help you when I pointed to Joan's deep significance for you, for what you need most now is not deep feelings, but comfortable feelings. The more comfortable you feel, the better you'll heal. If you feel comfortable with a date at the movies, the coffee shop and the supermarket, you'll grow more secure. Joan helps you, not necessarily because of the depth of your relationship, but because she allows you to feel so comfortable. The more you feel comfort, the more you'll know that rejection is not an absolute necessity. A new date may still be frightening for quite a while. But there will be hope, for you'll have more experience of feeling good with a woman.

Burt's reaction was complex. He was very moved by the message but, in the following session, asked to space out the meetings because he had become a bit pessimistic and wanted to leave women aside for a while and concentrate on his studies. The day after the critical intervention, he had dared, for the first time, to ask Joan to masturbate him, instead of trying as he always did to force orgasm coitally. He was badly disappointed, however, for though he was tremendously excited, he had failed to ejaculate. The therapist told him that sexual improvement would probably not come in a big bang of an orgasm that would change everything in one shot. Instead, he would probably grow more and more free, open, and excitable. He might have an orgasm, tomorrow or in a year, but nothing good would come from pushing hard against his physical responses. What mattered most now was his growing sense of comfort, and this might eventually bring a change in sexual functioning as well. It would be better, the therapist added, to continue meeting once a week for a while, so as to follow through with the change in the therapeutic dialogue that had been brought about by the consultation. If, after a couple of months, Burt still wanted to space out the meetings, it would be all right with her. Burt gladly agreed to this proposal and the therapy proceeded on a much better footing.

The hidden agenda in this case included the commonly held belief that patients with an apparently somatic problem must become aware of its psychological nature for a real psychotherapy to develop. With difficult (i.e., nonpsychologically-minded) patients, therapists often keep their psychological theory of causation to themselves, but their tacit belief comes across and the patient ends feeling charged with hypochondriasis, somatization, or malingering. This typical error can be prevented by the therapist's acceptance of the disturbance's physiological basis,* a step that almost invariably improves the therapeutic alliance. Patients do not rush to the conclusion that psychotherapy cannot help them. On the contrary, as with Burt, it becomes easier to focus on personal issues, for the patient is no longer proved wrong by acknowledging their relevance.

Case 11: The Computer Boy

Fabian, a 16-year-old boy, was referred to therapy by his parents because of memory blocks that were badly affecting his scholastic performance. He complained that sometimes he failed to answer a single question on an exam. His marks were uneven, high in math, perfect in computers, but very poor in the humanities. He not only forgot everything in literature and history: he hardly understood what was expected of him in these subjects.

---

*Even in the absence of medical findings, it is safer to assume that the patient is not "imagining" physical symptoms. Even in the clearest cases of psychologically triggered complaints, there must be a physical substratum that mediates the painful sensations.

The parents, both engineers, had moved to England for three years when Fabian was six. Although Fabian spoke Hebrew marvelously by then, once in England he went over to English completely, becoming fluent in a few months. The stay in England was remembered as good, but the return to Israel as very rough. Fabian went back to Hebrew slowly and never regained the articulateness he had once possessed. Socially also he had trouble adapting: he was a loner and, for a while, very aggressive with other kids. The parents described Fabian as a well disciplined but closed child, who could talk easily about sports and computers but never said a word about his troubles. The parents themselves were also quite guarded and responded laconically to the therapist's inquiries: the marital relationship was okay; Fabian's brother was okay; the two brothers managed okay together. They could supply some meager factual information, but subtler questions led nowhere.

With Fabian the therapist fared no better. He could tell what he had done the day before and what he had read in the newspaper. He performed well on objective tests, scoring high on the Wechsler and showing excellent spontaneous recall on the Bender. When told that his performance showed a good memory, Fabian said that he either remembered everything or nothing at all. The therapist asked how he studied for an exam and Fabian said that he read the material once. This, he considered, should suffice for perfect retrieval. That it sometimes did not, leading instead to no retrieval, baffled him.

His performance on projective tests was quite peculiar. He could not, for instance, make up a story for the TAT. When pressed for it, he would give a flow-chart in the form: "If the violin belongs to the boy, and if the parents want him to study, and he doesn't want to study, he is angry. If he wants to study, he is thinking about it. If the parents don't want him to study, and he wants to study, he is angy. If they don't want him to study, and he doesn't want to study, he is indifferent."

When asked about feelings or personal interactions, Fabian would lower his head and tense his arms, maintaining this posture for minutes, until the therapist interrupted him:

THERAPIST: So, what do you say?
FABIAN: I don't know.
THERAPIST: What are you thinking about?
FABIAN: Nothing.
THERAPIST: Why are your arms so tense?
FABIAN: I don't know.
THERAPIST: Tell me the first thing that comes to your mind.
FABIAN: Nothing.

The therapist tried to communicate with him through metaphors, with very little success. She asked him to draw a picture of his memory problem. Fabian drew a black circle. She asked him to draw a picture of how his problem might improve and he drew a white circle. She commented on Fabian's all-or-none thinking, interpreted his tenseness as anger, linked what was happening to the traumas he had suffered in the past, asked about dreams, asked for memories about England and his return, but to no avail. Only once did he acknowledge the presence of an emotion: he could recognize that he was angry when he played the flute, because the sound lost its smoothness. The therapist asked him if he thought the meetings were helping him. He did not think so. She felt just as blocked as Fabian and brought the case to consultation.

The therapist had conceptualized Fabian's problem as resulting from early deprivation in Fabian's relationship with his unemotional parents. These early experiences had been reactivated by the traumatic dislocations involved in the trip to England and the return to Israel. Fabian had reacted by massive repression, which affected the whole range of his memory, and by robot-like adaptation. Being a smoothly functioning machine was his defense and compensation for the barrenness of the home environment. Based on this analysis, the success or failure of therapy hinged on its ability to pierce the robotic armor and gain access to the frightening area of disowned feelings. Fabian was on his way to becoming a "normotic" personality (Bollas, 1987), that is, a person with a need to be completely desubjectified. He had to regain his disowned self or lose all hope for a real life.

This therapeutic agenda was not shared with Fabian. The therapist believed that the memory problem, which was the agreed target of therapy, could not be addressed except by dismantling the defense. Fabian would not accept the deeper agenda at this point, but there seemed to be no other way of attaining the symptomatic goal. Most group members agreed with the psychodynamic analysis but doubted whether getting in touch with the underlying feelings would help Fabian to function better on his exams. They asked themselves, however, whether treatment should not be pursued simply with the goal of helping Fabian become a fuller person. The unavowed means were thus valued more than the avowed end. Fabian probably saw where the therapy was heading, and disliked what he saw. In the course of the group discussion, it became clear that the hidden agenda was depriving the therapy of a common ground. The following message was therefore framed, to replace it with a shared agenda:

I have been thinking about what goes wrong with you in exams. You have been misusing your brain potential, because you think that memory is an all-or-none affair. You think that you either remember something or not, but memory works probabilistically. The process of remembering is tentative and includes an element of guessing. For instance, when you try to memorize a chapter in history, you first read it from beginning to end. This creates memory traces. At the time of the exam you are supposed to retrieve these traces, which are hidden among other traces. How can you get hold of the right traces? There is no sure way to land there straight. You must begin by making an initial guess, by striking in some direction. Such a guess has a probability, say, of thirty percent of hitting at the right traces. If you guessed right, you will remember more, for one trace leads to another. You may increase your initial probability of guessing right, however, if you have more memory traces to begin with. This is best achieved not simply by cramming more, but by studying the same material in different ways. Say that, besides reading the material, you also write down a summary. Now you have two kinds of traces, spread over different areas of your brain. The first set of traces goes to your "reading memory," the second to your "writing memory." The chances of getting hold of the right traces in the exam have now been raised to, say, fifty percent. If you add another set of traces, for instance, by reading the material to a tape-recorder and listening to it when you go for a walk or before you go to sleep, you create yet another set of traces, this time in your "speech and hearing memory." You may raise the probability of retrieval on and on, for instance, by doing questions and answers, by underlining the important parts in different colors, or by studying with someone else. Each new modality establishes a new kind of trace and the probability of success increases. It will never be a hundred percent, however, because there is always a chance that the noise in your brain—that is, other memory traces—may hide the signal during the exam.

I think that whenever I ask you a question that is probabilistic in nature, you get blocked, because you try to answer it in an all-or-none fashion. For instance, if I ask you: "How does your father feel about your school problem?" You act as if there is an all-or-none answer to this question. You lower your head and set your computer *running, but in vain, for this is a probabilistic question with probabilistic answers. If you begin by guessing around, you may find out that you know more than you think. I believe that if you could learn to answer in a probabilistic way, you would function better in exams and would be better able to understand what they want from you in probabilistic subjects such as literature.*

The brain acts like that in many areas. How do you succeed in reaching the cup upon the table? Your cerebellum makes a guess of the distance and launches your hand with a certain trajectory and momentum. The eyes and arm give feedback to the brain on the speed of the move, on its direction, and on the position of the glass. The brain corrects the initial trajectory according to the feedback. Without this correction, you would either miss the cup or topple it. If your brain refused to guess, waiting to hit at the right movement from start, your hand would never get going. In your exams, and when you lower your head and run your computer furiously, you do precisely that. You try to find the right movement with no guessing and no feedback.

I can try to help you, but I need your guidance. Whenever I see that, instead of starting with a guess, your computer starts on a crazy run, I will stop you, and ask for a probabilistic answer. We will soon know if the guess leads anywhere. Sometimes, however, we shall find that the question wasn't phrased in a way that your brain-computer could understand. You will then give me feedback and, with your help, I will rephrase the question so that your computer may deal with it. Eventually, you will learn how to rephrase by yourself the questions that you don't understand. This is a two-way deal: you will learn how to guess and I will learn how to rephrase my questions so as to fit your computer. We will both have to correct ourselves by feedback.

Fabian reacted positively and agreed forthwith to work with the therapist in preparing for an exam on Jewish history. Instead of trying to find the right answer, Fabian was to listen inwardly for a cue, which he should verbalize. This procedure helped him deal with questions that had previously baffled him, such as: "What was the attitude of the Lithuanians towards the followers of Hassidism?" After two sessions of this practice, Fabian surprised the therapist by talking spontaneously about problems at school and at home. He said that, in the past, when his brother or other kids teased him, he would react violently, but he had now stopped doing so, shutting up instead. The therapist said that this problem and the problem with exams were the two sides of the same coin: he either reacted totally or not at all, so that learning to function probabilistically in exams would teach him to do the same with other kids, and learning to deal more flexibly with them would help him function better in exams. He was using all-or-none responses, where a feedback-guided approach was required. Fabian listened and responded. Sometimes it was the therapist who corrected herself. The critical intervention had created a common language for this therapy.

STRATEGY, CONFLICT, AND DIALECTICS

Improving goals, strengthening alliances, negotiating obstacles, and mobilizing effort, at times become highly complex tasks, for the solution to one problem often engenders another. For instance: a once dependent wife becomes more autonomous but starts to feel lonely; a stormy adolescent calms down but stops painting; a married woman stops having affairs but grows fat. Sometimes, someone else pays the price. For instance: a young man breaks away from his controlling parents, but a sister is left to bear the brunt; the slaving wife and mother becomes a proud feminist, but her children and husband feel left in the lurch. The flip-side of adjustment is not always what was bargained for.

Strategy in psychotherapy must adapt itself to this eternal seasaw, in which all prizes have their prices, goals compete with goals, and actions provoke reactions. For this reason, therapeutic strategies are often antithetical in nature, progressing by seemingly contrary steps or displaying a pendular sequence of advance and retreat (Omer, 1992). Strategies that are built out of two apparently contrary movements, inducing change while at the same time fending off resistance, have been termed *dialectical* (Omer, 1991b). Let us review some brief illustrations.

Some family therapists have developed the strategy of *good therapist/bad therapist* (the one supportive and optimistic, the other critical and pessimistic) to neutralize resistance and increase motivation (Hoffman & Laub, 1986). An electively mute five-year-old girl, for instance, was faced with a bad therapist who said she was childish and stubborn, and bet a bag of candy that she would not talk to the teacher in kindergarten. The good therapist protested, telling the bad one that he had no right to talk like that to the girl. After the session, the good therapist winked to the girl conspiratorially and told her in a whisper that the bad therapist was wrong and would yet be sorry for what he had said. The bad therapist lost the bet and ended up by acknowledging that he had been taught a lesson.

In another dialectical strategy, the same marital therapist gives contrary prescriptions, to each spouse, one straightforward and one paradoxical. For instance, while the husband is trained in self-control to avoid quarreling, the wife is paradoxically enjoined to continue teasing him, so as to help him exercise his new skills. Or, while a dependent wife is enjoined to do things by herself, the withdrawn husband is paradoxically told to withstand the urge to be nice to her, so as to help her develop her autonomy (Lange, 1989). The paradoxical prescription dulls the edge of the offensive spouse's behavior (for one cannot offend by request), thereby increasing the victimized spouse's readiness to cooperate with the prescription.

Dialectical strategies may progress by an alternation of the two contraposed movements, as in the *two-chair technique* (Perls, 1969) and the *odd and even days ritual* (Boscolo et al., 1987). In the two-chair technique, the client is enjoined to role-play first one and then the other of two contrary tendencies, before "owning up" to both. In the odd and even days ritual, the spouses are told to rule on alternate days of the week—the husband on Mondays, Wednesdays, and Fridays and the wife on Tuesdays, Thursdays, and Saturdays. On Sundays, the couple is to act "spontaneously." When successful, these techniques bring about a new synthesis between the opposing trends.

At times, two mutually exclusive goals may be pursued together, as illustrated by the *double-advance technique* (Omer & Alon, 1989). This strategy consists in choosing a course of action which advances both goals at once, leaving the choice to a later point in time. For instance, a young woman came to therapy because her longtime boyfriend kept postponing the decision to get married because he was not emotionally ready. When pressed by her, he decided to start individual therapy (of the interminable kind) so as to work at the roots of his indecisiveness. She became furious and left him. But then, she repented that she had not waited a little longer. She went back to him, but became angry and wanted to leave again. A step in any direction would thus lead to an impulse in the other. The therapist told her to set a date in the future when she was to leave him if, by then, he had not decided to marry her. Until that date she was to stay with him unconditionally, without telling him about her date or her decision. In the meantime she was to prepare for the separation by cultivating friendships, family relationships, personal appearance, career, hobbies, etc. Her new behavior worried the boyfriend no end, while at the same time making her more independent.*

In a well-known variety of dialectical strategy, the therapist fans up the patient's dysfunctional expectations, so as to better refute them therapeutically. Such is *the corrective emotional experience* made famous by Alexander and French (1946). For example, a young man had learned to suppress his dependent strivings, which in his family of origin had led invariably to rejection. As a defense, he developed, instead, a blatant self-sufficiency that alienated others and turned his life into a lonely struggle against growing odds. His female therapist nourished his subdued dependent yearnings, thus exacerbating his expectations of rejection. When, in a crisis, these negative expectations reached their highest pitch, she reacted by trebling the frequency of sessions and instructing the patient's wife to be especially caring and protective towards him. This corrective experience functioned as a critical intervention that was, in turn, followed by a stage of normal therapy in which the new learnings were gradually made conscious and stable.

Smooth successful vignettes, however, give us no feel for the price and the grimness that may, at times, be exacted. The following example should redress the balance and counter the impression that strategic planning always equals elegant ease.

Case 13: Order and Rebellion

After stealing money from his mother's purse, Moish, a teenager from a religious Jewish family, jumped out of his window, took a taxi to a discotheque, spent the Sabbath evening in forbidden dancing, and was finally caught by his father while trying to climb back into his room in the early morning hours,

---

*In two out of three similar cases in which this technique was applied, the boyfriend decided to marry within a few months; in one, the young woman left the boyfriend for good, long before the stipulated date.

stinking of cigarettes. There was hardly a sin that he hadn't committed in the course of a few hours.*

Lately, Moish had clashed with his father about his religious school, which he wanted to leave. He was failing in his studies, had often stayed home under feeble pretenses, and was a complete stranger to the school's sober atmosphere. His father, a well-known figure in religious circles, would not even consider Moish's desires: if he failed in that school, he would be sent to a no less orthodox one. The mother was soft to Moish, but he was very rough in return, often shutting her up with offensive epithets. He also extorted money from her for fancy sneakers and jeans. After the discotheque incident, Moish declared that he was no longer religious: he would stop frequenting the synagogue and wearing a yarmulka.

Moish wasn't the first to go wild at home. His elder brother, aged 22, had turned secular two years before and lived at home without any contact with the other family members, including Moish. He was an heretic and an outcast. Initially, the father had raged and fumed, but he shifted from overt hostility to ostracism when physical violence erupted.

Without compromise and dialogue the family was in danger of disintegrating. Moish and his father, however, were in no mind for either: the father demanded unconditional obedience and Moish declared that he would not be compelled. The therapist might well sound the need for flexibility: nobody listened. Soon, there might be one more outcast in another room of the ever more fragmented home. The therapist, a religious woman from the community clinic, brought the case to consultation after three sessions.

The group agreed that both sides had to change before they were ready for compromise. One of the participants proposed

---

*Traveling, smoking, and spending money are forbidden on the Sabbath. Stealing and disco dancing are forbidden everyday.

a double-stage dialectical strategy: in the first stage, the father would be helped to put up a very tough disciplinary fight (the mother seemed so weak and detached that only her passive cooperation seemed obtainable). The very hardships of this stage should be conducive to the next: softened by the sweat and tears exacted by the battle, both sides would hopefully become amenable to dialogue.

The father was phoned at work and asked whether he was willing to fight for his principles and for his son's future. He answered enthusiastically in the affirmative, whereupon he was asked to give absolute top priority to the project for the duration of one month. He would have to spend many hours a day on "fighting duty" and would need the help of a relative, preferably a strong one (the father was of small build). He said that his brother-in-law, who lived in the same building, would agree to lend a hand. The therapist told him gravely that "one hand" would not be enough, and a meeting was called with both parents and the brother-in-law. The school's principal, who had often collaborated with the clinic in the past, was made a party to the plan. The first stage was thus launched with the backing of a network of alliances.

For the coming month, Moish would be taken to school by the father, who in addition would phone the school three times every morning and step in at least once again at different hours, so as to make his presence felt. Furthermore, the father would come home earlier from work, so as to be available on the home front. A policy of strict control over money was instituted, to prevent filching. New locks were installed on Moish's window and on the front door, and the new keys were carefully guarded. The mother's acquiescence was guaranteed by making Moish's offensive behavior towards her into one of the program's chief issues. Whenever Moish screamed at her or called her names, the father was to call the brother-in-law and both would take Moish by force to his room, pin him down to his bed and keep him immobilized for two hours. No explanations were to be forwarded. The therapist, the consultant, and the school principal would be on call around the clock.

Initially, Moish put up little resistance. He and his father even developed some form of dialogue on their trips to the school (the father had been expressly instructed to avoid all sermonizing). When the pinning-down job was first applied, however, Moish raised such hell that a neighbor called the police. A cop, who was on duty in the area, arrived in a few minutes, interrupting the proceedings. The cop, who knew the family, told Moish that if he wished he could come to the police station and file a complaint against his father, an option that Moish chose not to follow.

Moish began to react positively. For over a week he became talkative and seemed surprisingly calmer. One evening, however, he came home with a radio he had bought from a friend. His father asked him how much he had paid and decided that he could not keep it. Moish was peremptorily ordered to return the radio immediately to his friend. This high-handed use of authority, on an issue that was not perceived as legitimate by Moish, provoked a backlash. He stayed out for the whole night. After a fruitless search, the father called the therapist and the school principal, the therapist called the head of the clinic and the head of the clinic called the consultant (myself). Nobody slept. Moish returned in the morning and was immediately pinned down, this time with no resistance. An emergency session with the parents was called by the therapist and the following message was framed to be solemnly delivered to Moish: "You did wrong not to return the radio last evening and even more wrong not to come back. But we understand that you felt humiliated. This was not our purpose. We do not wish to humiliate you and will do our best that this shall not happen again. You are a citizen in this house and, as a citizen, you have to abide by its rules and laws. We will uphold the rules and the laws, but without humiliation. You will be a full citizen with full duties and full honor." The therapeutic leitmotif became, "boundaries without humiliation." After this crisis no further coercion was required. The hurt and the scare had taken their toll and, at the end of three weeks, Moish and his father were ready to compromise.

The father agreed to send Moish to a secular school and Moish agreed to keep all religious ordinances. From then on, Moish accompanied his father to the synagogue every Saturday. There was one more crisis, a few months later. One night, Moish became extremely upset and started screaming that he wanted to be sent to jail or to a mental hospital. The parents were very scared, but the brother took Moish out for a ride and calmed him down. The next day Moish was still very agitated and the brother took him to a psychiatrist. He was given tranquilizers, which he took for a short while. The crisis brought about a rapprochement between Moish and his brother and for a while it seemed that the brother might also find his way back to the family. Unfortunately, this did not happen, and Moish's brother soon resumed his position as the family outcast. The therapist was informed of these events only much later, during a follow-up. She was also told that Moish was happy with the new school and was closer to his father.

CONCLUSION: THE STRATEGIC SIDE OF PSYCHOTHERAPY

The career of strategic concepts in psychotherapy parallels, in time and scope, that of narrative ones. Both owe their origin to the pluralist revolution. In the era of the one true theory and the one true method, there was not much place for choosing goals and means. There was one true goal and one right way. There was also little room for choosing allies: the client and the patient were viewed as one and the same, for any attempt to achieve change away from the true locus of pathology was deemed preposterous. The pluralist revolution underscored the pragmatic nature of the definition of goals, means, and the client system. Furthermore, the demise of absolute systems has made us wary of lengthy and unconstrained therapies: we must be patient and long-suffering when there is one royal way to a unique goal; when byways wink from every side, we grow restless. The same is true for monetary limitations: the free market of therapeutic approaches has made us keenly aware of costs. The pluralist revolution is thus social no less than theoretical. In a competitive world, devoid of absolute assumptions, choice becomes all-pervasive and strategy inescapable.

5

REPAIRING THE

THERAPEUTIC RELATIONSHIP

THE QUALITY OF THE therapeutic relationship has been shown to be the best predictor of therapeutic outcome (see Horvath & Symond, 1991, for a review). Many therapists, in fact, seem to believe that the relationship is all: if therapy goes wrong, check the relationship; if right, thank the relationship. If the relationship is as it should be, knowledge and technical skill lead to success; if not, no amount of knowledge and technical skill will suffice. Critical interventions are pretty fireworks if the relationship is good; obnoxious sound and fury if it is bad. Theory and technique are thus no more than embellishments upon the real curative factor: the relationship.

This position is rather simplistic, however, for the quality of the relationship is not independent of the skill with which the therapist handles the case. A good therapeutic alliance rests not only on empathy and acceptance but also on the therapist's provision of helpful comments and hopeful options (Crits-Christoph, Barber, & Kurcias, 1993). If these are lacking, the alliance stays lame.

If the establishment of a good relationship is a matter for professional skill, so much more so the repair of a damaged one. The belief that to improve a damaged relationship it is enough to clarify feelings is illusory. The relationship grows sour because of what the therapist does, or fails to do, and unless the ineffective or offensive acts are spotted and made good, emotional awareness will not solve the problem.

Still, repairing the relationship might be a job too delicate for the bangs of critical interventions. As Safran has argued (Safran, in press; Safran, Crocker, McMain, & Murray, 1990), the treatment of ruptures in the alliance requires continuous watchfulness for incipient breaches that are still tractable, before they grow into full-blown chasms. This process of constant vigilance and repair is all the more worthwhile because the ruptures are living examples of the very problems that poison the patient's interpersonal relations. Investigating the relationship and keeping it in good order is thus not only a condition for therapy but the gist of its work. From this perspective, major impasses will not arise and critical interventions will have no place in a well-conducted therapy: daily weeding of our therapeutic garden will keep it free from baobabs.

Numerous patients (and not a few therapists), however, object to this ongoing scrutiny of the relationship, deeming it evasive of the real tasks of therapy. Furthermore, even among those who are amenable to it, many fail to profit. Focusing on the relationship may well be the royal therapeutic game for some, but it is a wild goose chase for others. Whichever way we choose for doing normal therapy, impasses are bound to arise and, at times, to prove refractory to the therapy's usual procedures. A critical intervention may then be required, often with the very goal of releasing the therapy from an unproductive focus on the relationship.

According to the impasse model, the first step in repairing the therapeutic relationship is to identify the therapist's beliefs and attitudes that may have contributed to the dysfunctional interaction. Therapists find it hard to do this by themselves, not only because they are immersed in their own perspectives, but also because the offending beliefs and attitudes are often viewed as almost synonymous with the psychotherapeutic creed itself. Consider the following typical therapeutic assumptions:

(1) *The patient needs the symptom.* Although hypotheses about the functional significance of symptoms may play a constructive role in therapy, they may also become tools for hammering patients. Interactional deadlock often arises when the therapist says or implies that the patient has a vested interest in the symptom. In the therapist's eyes this is the bitter pill that the patient must swallow in order to improve. The patient, however, feels unjustly blamed. The tone of the therapist's delivery may often, in itself, justify the patient. But even when the therapist succeeds in conveying the message empathically, a whiff of superiority may leak through.

(2) *The patient wants easy relief, not real change.* This therapeutic belief comes into play whenever patients complain that progress is not quick enough or that its price is higher than they had bargained for. "Change" is capitalized by therapists: it is a weighty, costly, and most estimable process. Easy change, light change, and symptomatic change stand low in the therapist's esteem, and patients who desire these cheap substitutes find themselves humbled and rebuked. They may protest, or meekly lower their heads, but the resentment that breeds under the surface takes its inevitable toll on the relationship.

(3) *The patient's physical symptoms are psychological.* Telling this to patients is almost invariably a mistake. Therapists often misuse the term "psychosomatic" to denote entities that are only psychological, that is, deprived of physiological reality. The therapeutic alliance is damaged as a result, for the patient feels the trouble in the body, not in the head.

Body-mind stalemates are often engendered even before psychotherapy begins. The patient goes from one physician to another and is told that there is nothing wrong with the body. Psychotherapy is then recommended as a wastebasket. The therapist who buys into the physicians' verdict pays a price, for pain is pain, choking is choking, and tachycardia is tachycardia, even when psychological processes are also involved.

(4) *Feeling is more important than thinking.* For most therapists, a language that is emotionally charged is not only more informative but also more valuable and real than a more rational one. Feelings are prized as worthier than thoughts (or even acts), and awareness of feelings is viewed as an indisputable asset. Patients, however, do not necessarily agree with this appraisal, and this should not be proof of their immaturity or unfitness. Among the many slurs that we cast on patients, disparaging their intellectual "defenses" is among the most ubiquitous. The capacity for critical thinking and abstract conceptualization is a major achievement, and we should beware of shrugging it off.

(5) *The patient's self-demands are too strict.* Therapists are often apostles of permissiveness and self-tolerance. Rigid superegos and perfectionistic demands are the profession's bugbears. Indeed, some patients are cruelly self-demanding, but still, our easy messages of self-tolerance may clash with their dearest values. We are professionally biased towards weakness. An appreciative recognition of the value of strict,

self-imposed ideals is not taught in our schools, and the scope of therapeutic empathy is narrowed as a result.

These are only some of the impasse-prone beliefs that are held almost unconsciously by psychotherapists.* The way out of many a stuck therapy lies in recognizing these beliefs for what they are: working assumptions to be checked against their influence on the therapeutic relationship and process. Many of the critical interventions in this book may be understood as rites by which the therapist abjures such beliefs when they give rise to ineffective interactions.

INEFFECTIVE INTERACTIONS

In a reciprocal interaction, each side mirrors the other's behavior in a mutual escalation, as when hostility is followed by hostility and avoidance by avoidance. In a complementary interaction, each side provokes the other's opposite responses, as when prodding leads to withdrawal, encouragement to discouragement. Reciprocal and complementary interactions (when negatively toned) may lead to extremely recalcitrant vicious circles (Bateson, 1972a, 1972b; Kiesler, 1982, 1983).

Therapeutic impasses are characterized by negative complementarity or reciprocity, and their resolution requires nonreciprocal or noncomplementary responses. In the following case, I shall focus on a particular kind of complementarity, in which the therapist's capacity to act is progressively curtailed by fears that the patient may drop out, break down, or commit suicide. As the therapist becomes more and more narrowly

---

*Some additional examples would be: "The past determines all," "The past is irrelevant," "The parents are to blame," "Symptoms are not important," "Symptoms are all," "Lack of material shows lack of motivation," "The whole family has to change," "Progress is dangerous for the patient," and "The patient is not ready for autonomy."

cornered, the patient's threat (intended or not) gains power and the therapist's options become ever more constricted.

Case 13: The Cornered Therapist

A widowed mother came to treatment because of her eldest daughter, Eva (aged 21), who had not left the house for more than six months. Except for shouting offenses and commands, she had not spoken to anybody in the family (mother and two younger brothers, aged 14 and 13) for years. She would stay in her room most of the time, coming out only to eat or watch television. Anyone who dared to stay in the room when Eva watched television had to maintain strict silence. Even then, she would wrap herself up in a protective cloak and sit right before the screen, shutting herself off from the others' presence. By screaming and throwing things about, Eva had forced the younger brother to stop playing the piano. She never ate with the family, keeping a shelf of her own in the refrigerator. Neither did she launder her clothes with those of the family. When she washed the floor of her room, she left the dirty water in her mother's room, which adjoined hers.

Eva's behavior at home contrasted sharply with her behavior at school, the army, and the youth movement, places where she had always been found pleasant and sociable. By shutting herself up at home, Eva effectively cut herself off from all life areas in which she had behaved appropriately.

There were other problems in the family. Ever since she had become a widow (11 years previously), the mother had been extremely protective of her children. Sleeping at friends' homes, going to camp, even going on tours with the school were out of the question. The mother did the housework all by herself and the children's only duty was to study. None of them (until Eva went to the army) had ever gone shopping or traveled alone. The mother never mentioned their father. When asked why she kept them thus, she gave two answers: she did not trust them and she wanted to keep them from pain.

The mother had been to four therapists on account of Eva's strange behavior, but Eva had invariably refused to come to even a single session. The present therapist (the fifth) accomplished the impossible and succeeded in bringing Eva in. She courted Eva by coaching the mother on better ways of treating her. For instance, all hostile communications were to be replaced by friendly ones. The mother was to write short cordial notes to Eva, such as "Good appetite!" when she served her a meal and "I hope you enjoy it!" when she brought her the weekly woman's magazine. The therapist also sent Eva short reports on the family sessions. Eva read the reports (as became known later) and tore them up, leaving the shreds at her doorsill. Needless to say, she never answered. The estrangement at home remained, but the aggressiveness subsided. Eva stopped screaming and throwing things about. At this stage, the therapist took the plunge and phoned her. Eva was surprisingly agreeable. To the therapist's request for her help with the family therapy, Eva replied that she was not interested. She did not care about the family, but only about herself. After a few phone conversations, however, Eva agreed to an appointment, keeping the right to cancel it if she felt like it. She came to the clinic alone.

Eva refused to talk about the family. She had erased them from her life. The therapist agreed that the conversations should deal only with what mattered to Eva. Whenever the slightest allusion was made to the family, Eva would stop the therapist, saying: "You see, there you go again, like all psychologists."

She told the therapist that she loved television serials and fantasized about living the life of a successful and beautiful career woman or becoming the bosom friend of some glamorous star. She dreamt about a lover and about getting rich. In a slightly more realistic vein she would talk about finding "a friend for life." She would end the session by saying, "You can't help me to get these things, can you? So what's the use of talking?" The therapist replied that they could work to bring some of the dreams closer to reality. Eva said she did not want to work. Actually, she said, she would do nothing that was expected from her, such as studying or working. At the end of each session, there would be a discussion about whether to schedule another meeting. Eva would say she needed no help. In the end, she would allow herself to be persuaded, but she always kept the right to cancel the session if she felt like it.

Meanwhile, work with the mother and the younger brothers proceeded on different lines. Encouraged by the therapist, the mother broke her silence about the father, showed pictures of him to the two sons, told them stories about him, and took them to visit the grave. She also dared to make demands of them and started to give them more freedom. In a few weeks they were doing more on their own than she had bargained for.

In Eva's life there was also change: she started to go out and meet with friends from the youth movement in her neighborhood. The rudimentary therapeutic relationship, however, seemed extremely precarious. The therapist was never sure whether Eva would keep the next appointment. If any of the forbidden issues (such as the father's death, or the mother-daughter relationship) were as much as hinted at, she would insinuate that she might stop coming. Avoiding them, however, did not secure Eva's cooperation: she kept saying that the sessions were "nice" but that the therapist could not help her. After seven sessions, the therapist feared that her slightest move might shatter the fragile alliance. The therapist felt she had to escape her cornered position or give up her professional leverage altogether. She brought the case for consultation and the following message was framed, to be delivered to Eva, orally and in writing:

You are right in wanting so badly to separate from your family. For you, the family is a sinking bog, ugly and dead, and you can only wish for something wholly different. Your desire to care only for yourself is a healthy one, and it should be cherished. However, you cannot escape your prison without being well acquainted with it. You cannot get out of the swamp without a map. You cannot rebel without knowing full well what you are rebelling against. By refusing to give a thought to the family that you want to escape, you only increase its hold upon you. You may end up incarcerated within the house, totally dependent on those whom you wish most to avoid. Your mother's message that the world outside is a dangerous place will then be fully realized in your life. Indeed, you are slowly becoming the most loyal of your mother's children. On the surface, you are rebellious. On a deeper level, however, your mother's voice goes with you and you live by it.

You asked me, rhetorically, if I could help you fulfill your dreams. I think I can. I don't have a magic wand, but I can help you break out of your jail and live independently. You must, however, allow me to help you. I think you could leave your house and find a place of your own, with your share of your father's life insurance. You should exorcize your mother's voice and I believe I can help you achieve this. I think I can help you find your own friends and, eventually, a friend for life. I think we can do this, but you must help me. We must have sessions once a week and I must be allowed to talk freely, even about the family, so that you may find your release. I am offering you partnership in a plan of escape. Please, don't answer me now. Think about this for a week, and we shall talk about it then.

Eva wanted to give a negative answer on the spot, but the therapist stopped her and phoned her a week later. Eva did not think that the therapist could help her. The therapist might be right in the things she said, but they were irrelevant at the moment. In a trembling voice, Eva confessed that leaving the house even for a short while or boarding a bus was a veritable ordeal for her, to say nothing about living by herself. She would not come to the clinic again, for the meetings were useless. The critical intervention had failed miserably and the therapist was left with a broken alliance, without even a place in the corner. The relationship, however, might still be resuscitated.

BROKEN RELATIONSHIPS

An unexplained dropout, an abrupt ending by a disappointed client, or a phasing out of therapy after an agonizing stalemate causes damage as well as unpleasantness. For the patient, a broken relationship is one more failure in a chain. It breeds distrust and blackens the good sides of the abandoned therapy. A bad ending not only stops therapeutic interventions but is a harmful intervention in itself.

Therapists universally acknowledge the importance of a good termination. Separation unleashes strong feelings that, if wisely handled, may consolidate and enhance therapeutic achievements — so much so that termination is sometimes seen as constituting the major mission of psychotherapy (Mann, 1973).

In the considerable literature on termination problems, the assumption is always that the therapeutic dialogue is still on. Dealing with a broken relationship presents a different challenge. The therapist, for one, may not be able to invite the patient for another session: feelings are touchy after the rupture, and the offer of a meeting might be interpreted as an attempt to renew the very relation from which the patient has chosen to break away. If the meeting does take place, all the negative expectations, feelings, and reactions that characterized the therapy's final stage threaten to rise again. Any attempt to mend the breach might find the participants enmeshed in the very tangles that led to the break. In these circumstances, an extraordinary letter might offer a less threatening path for bridging the gap (Omer, 1991a). Such an epistolary critical intervention was developed in a new consultation concerning Eva.

Case 13: The Cornered Therapist (Continued)

The group attributed the previous failure to an underestimation of Eva's crippling fears. Her reaction to the critical message showed her to be at least as anxious as she was rebellious. Eva had been perceived as able to fend for herself (after all, she had successfully concluded her army service), but apparently she did not share this positive view of her abilities.

The strategy, in the first intervention, had been rather combative: Eva was invited to set out on a crusade for independence. She reacted complementarily, disclosing, for the first time, her sense of inner weakness. The new critical message should build on this new note, legitimizing Eva's sense of insecurity and offering her a more traditional patient role. The therapeutic narrative that had guided the previous intervention had cast Eva in the role of heroine. Maybe a narrative describing her as victim would fare better.* For once, "psychiatrizing" the case might be the right thing to do.

The previous critical intervention had been followed by one good sign: Eva called the therapist on her own, a few days after their previous phone conversation, to thank her sincerely for her efforts and for the sessions. Unfortunately, however, she could not accept the therapist's offer. By this time, the second consultation had already taken place, and the therapist told Eva that she had thought a lot about her in the meantime and had sent her a letter to share the new thoughts with her. Here is the letter:

Dear Eva,

I think I know what was wrong in my proposal. I was blind to how helpless, frightened and paralyzed you may feel. This mistake made me offer you something quite impossible: a battle plan for fighting your way out of prison and gaining independence. Those are lofty goals and

---

*Nothing like breaking one's own principles once in a while.

you would surely want them. But how could you? How could you go to war without feeling that you had the strength and the skill to undertake even a fraction of a fraction of what would be needed? No wonder that when I made you my offer, you knew from the very start what your answer would be.

I want to share my thoughts with you so that, at times of despair, you may weigh them carefully. You suffer from a well-known problem. Your feeling of being unable to go out, to ride a bus, to walk freely, and to be alone outside is called "agoraphobia." This condition can be treated. There are two ways of treating it, and even people who had been closed up for twenty years and more have been helped out of it. The first way is a training program: you can be taught how to cope with the fear gradually, expanding your ability to move around and learning ways to deal with the anxiety. Within a short period of training, people with agoraphobia attain a freedom of movement they couldn't have dreamed of before. The second way is based on a non-addictive medication that reduces the anxiety and sense of paralysis. It is possible to do both at once, for with the help of the medication, the training advances much more easily. If you wish, I can guide you through the training and put you in touch with a physician for the medication.

Perhaps the time is not ripe to renew our meetings. My mistake still rings in my ears (I hope it does not ring so badly in yours). I don't want you to feel that I expect a decision from you now. But I do want to allow myself the right to phone you again in a few weeks, and ask you how you feel about the treatment options that I have described to you. I will honor your "no" and rejoice in your "yes." But even if you say "no" I will still call again, hoping that, sometime, you will have had enough of despair. Of course, you can call me anytime.

When Eva was called a couple of weeks later she talked, for the first time, about how much she suffered. She was terribly lonely and wanted nothing more than a close friend with whom she could share her life. Her fears of going out, however, were stronger than her suffering. She felt too weak to go through the training. Medication offered no alternative because, in the end, she would have to go out on her own and suffer the pain anyhow. She had never sounded so frail and poignant.

Although this was a far cry from Eva's original cavalier attitude towards the therapist, it was still not a working relationship. Eva expressed her pain but was not yet ready for a joint endeavor. The therapist still felt at a loss as to how to proceed. The case was therefore brought to a third consultation.

This time, a home visit was decided upon. The group felt that Eva's reaction made it worthwhile to risk an active attempt to engage her. The home visit would constitute a bid for a different relationship, one in which Eva would be encouraged, temporarily, to lean upon the therapist (DaVerona & Omer, 1993). This is what she was to be told at the home visit:

I came to see you at home because I felt that, by starting where you feel safe, we would have the best chance of success. I think, Eva, that the two sources of your suffering are closely linked. You suffer, in the first place, from an inability to go out, a sense of insecurity, and a feeling that the world is a dangerous and hostile place; you also suffer from a sense of aloneness, of being disconnected, of having no one close whom you can trust. The two problems are deeply linked: in your fear of going out, you express your sense of being disconnected. Without a feeling of closeness, we feel unprotected in the world and are safe only deep within our caves. When you try to go out, you feel even more detached, abandoned, and alone. We all need the inner presence of someone who isn't

*physically there. If, with my help, you could feel less
alone in your pain, you would be less afraid of moving
around; on the other hand, in learning to move with my
help, you will feel less detached and unprotected.*

*I want to take you out. I want us to leave the house
and plan together where we will go for our training. Once
there, we will move apart, but only for a few minutes,
just for as long as you feel safe. We will then meet again.
All the time of our short separation, you will know that I
will be waiting for you. You will know that, as you move
about, we will not be going further apart, but coming
closer together. You will discover a new kind of safety
and you will make progress by learning to feel secure
about my presence.*

*If you feel pessimistic and hopeless, you should know
that this is part of your condition. People with this problem always feel pessimistic, for optimism is the sense that
there is somebody out there and that the world is no
longer strange and hostile. It would be too hard to do this
on your own, perhaps impossible. I don't expect you to
be enthusiastic. I only want you to allow me to come next
week at this same time, and guide you.*

This intervention, unfortunately, could not be executed as
planned. Eva canceled the home visit one day before it was
scheduled: she felt it was useless. The therapist modified the
message and sent it by mail, but with disappointing results.
Eva still expressed gratitude, but refused to give the therapist
a chance. She continued to go out occasionally, but only to
places she knew very well, such as the youth movement or her
grandparents'. The home atmosphere also improved a bit; she
even went shopping with her mother a few times. Otherwise,
she remained a recluse. The consultant, the therapist, and the
group felt that all the critical interventions they could dream
of would not make Eva budge.

THE THERAPIST'S EMOTIONAL
REACTIONS TO THE PATIENT

The group consultational setting is less well suited than that of individual supervision for examining the therapist's emotional reactions and their interplay with the patient's: time and privacy are essential to this task. At times, however, the therapist's feelings towards the patient dwell glaringly at the very core of the impasse triangle, exercising a blocking or disruptive influence on the relationship. A critical intervention must then be devised, which is aimed at the therapist no less than the patient.

Case 14: The White Angel

Abe and Sara came to treatment after Sara found out, by peeping into their elder daughter's diary, that she had stolen money from the pupils' common fund at school and did not even feel guilty about it. The family (parents and two daughters, aged 16 and 14) was very religious and lived in a religious (Jewish) neighborhood. At the parents' request, the therapist agreed not to mention the stealing so as not to disclose the mother's indiscretion.

The therapist, a woman of 45, described Abe as very handsome, intelligent, and charismatic. Furthermore, he was highly motivated for therapy and talked openly about his feelings, whereas Sara was suspicious and domineering. These impressions found an echo in the daughters' feelings: both were crazy about the father but viewed the mother as impossibly demanding. One of Sara's most unpopular traits was her stinginess: the girls' weekly allowance was much smaller than that of their girlfriends. On this score, Sara made herself unpleasant with the therapist too, by haggling (successfully) about the fee and always paying with postdated checks, in spite of the fact that Abe held a well-paid position as a managing engineer.

Sara said that the family had been badly shaken by a crisis they had undergone three years previously: Abe had had an affair with Sara's cousin. When the affair exploded, Sara had considered a divorce, but had decided, in the end, to stay with the marriage. This was discussed in front of the daughters, who were well acquainted with all the sordid details of the case.

Ever since the affair, Sara controlled all of Abe's movements. He had to report continuously on his whereabouts and to turn over all cash, checks, and credit cards to Sara. This surveillance was about all there was to their relationship. Abe thought that until the marital issue were brought to treatment, the family would remain doomed. Sara believed that the damage was irreparable and that psychologists were useless.

The therapist thought it crucial to gain Sara's cooperation. Sara would usually open the session by declaring that the situation was hopeless and that nothing could be done. The therapist would empathize with Sara's feelings and Sara would gradually soften and agree to cooperate, for the session. This initial interchange would take a while, for Sara did not relent easily. The sessions therefore tended to become longer, lasting sometimes over two hours. Sara would pay for one hour, complain about the price, and continue to declare the therapy useless.

In an attempt to overcome Sara's reluctance, the therapist decided to address her hurt more cogently. She phoned Abe and told him that in the coming session he would be called upon to confess his errors, ask Sara's forgiveness, and offer reparation. Abe played his part feelingly and convincingly. He declared that his betrayal of Sara had been the worst thing he had ever done, that he knew he had hurt her irreparably, and that he couldn't ever express contrition and repentance enough. When the therapist urged Abe to address Sara directly, he burst into tears and told Sara that he had destroyed her love and trust, and betrayed the children no less than her. He concluded that he would do anything in his power to make reparation for even a share of the damage he had caused. He begged her to forgive him, if not for himself, for the sake of their children. Sara was deeply touched. She followed suit and confessed to the daughters that she had wronged them in treating them as she did. The elder daughter was almost caught in the confessional mood. She said that she also had things that weighed on her conscience and that she hoped the time would come when she would share them with the parents.

Sara and Abe felt that this session signaled a beginning thaw in their estrangement. No changes, however, transpired in Sara's domineering behavior. She maintained a reign of terror in matters of housekeeping and a spartan attitude toward all pleasures. She was the guardian of the family's religion and morals.

In the course of three sessions with the couple, the therapist found some chinks in Sara's monolith of law and order. She had bought a VCR and ordered tapes from a shop outside their neighborhood. This unconventional step for a religious family was kept secret from guests. If the daughters' friends became inquisitive, they were to say that the VCR belonged to Abe's work. Sara also enjoyed a woman's magazine that was considered inappropriate for religious women. She hid it within a Talmud volume. The therapist tried to connect this double standard morality to the daughter's stealing and lying. Sara, however, balked at this line. The therapist pushed, feeling that unless Sara gave up her rigid, and in no small measure hypocritical, prudishness, nothing would change. Sara began to lose interest in the therapy. The alliance that had been so laboriously built was wobbling and the therapist brought the case for consultation.

The therapist sounded extremely angry. She found Sara's double standard disgusting, was exasperated with her stinginess, and thought her most ungrateful. She had tried to raise the issue of her fees in a phone conversation with Abe, who said that she should definitely be reimbursed for the longer

sessions, but added that Sara held the purse strings. The therapist was also angry about Sara's control of the sessions and
right of veto upon what issues could be raised. She felt that
Sara was entangling the therapy in the same net of limitations
and cover-ups that was smothering the family.

The group helped the therapist to see how she had unwittingly abetted Sara's behavior, by failing to draw up a clear
contract from start. Furthermore, in identifying herself with
Abe and holding Sara responsible for the family's problems,
she had become drawn into the family pattern. Like Abe and
the children, she blamed Sara and did things behind her back.
In her secret phone conversations with Abe, she had established a coalition that isolated Sara even more.

To repair the therapeutic relationship, the therapist would
have to stop behaving as if she were Sara's victim and start
viewing Abe in a more balanced way. An alliance with the
couple should replace the coalition with Abe. This change in
the therapy should be directed at a parallel development in
the family: an alliance between Abe and Sara should replace the
unhealthy coalition between Abe and the daughters. With this
purpose, the following message was delivered to Abe and Sara:

*Sara, though I could understand your suffering, it took
me a long time to make out your emotional role in the
family: you are in charge of duty and morality; the fun,
you leave to Abe and the children. You make all the unpopular decisions and take upon yourself the opprobium
that such a role must inevitably incur. You manage everything with strictness and, as a result, you become the
family's bad person. You do all the dirty work, and are
blamed and disliked in return. Abe, in contrast, becomes
the nice guy who makes no demands. The children only
want to be with him and steal some hours of pleasure
behind your back. Because you take all the blackness
upon yourself, Abe can feel very good about himself. Abe*

feels light and pleasant before the children and before the world. You help him to become the family's white angel. In addition, everybody, except you, can be quite free from the burden of conscience. They say to themselves: "Mother holds the reins, sets the rules, commands, checks and exacts performance. We don't have to worry: she worries. So how can we have some more fun?" A pleasure-seeking underground evolves. Nobody feels guilty. You are the family conscience. Your daughter can steal without feeling really bad about it. You feel bad, instead. In the past, Abe could be unfaithful without feeling very bad about it. And who knows what is still brewing? Whatever it may be, you are the one who is sure to feel bad about it.

You pay a terrible price for your role. You get all the blows and Abe gets all the strokes. And as if this were not enough, you end up losing control of things, which are done more and more behind your back. You lost control over your husband, you lost control over your daughter, and you are probably losing control in many areas that you don't know of.

What can you do about this? Could you abandon the role of family manager and family conscience? Probably not. You cannot simply waive the responsibility. You don't do these things out of pleasure—you feel that they are forced upon you. Maybe all you can do is know your role in the family and the price you are paying. You allow the others to feel good about themselves, you launder the family conscience, but you end up isolated and vilified.

As for you, Abe, you collaborate with this situation. By being the white angel, doing only the nice things, being in charge of the fun, you leave all the dirt to Sara. She has to be bad because you are so good. Even with me, she haggles and you make a sorry face, meaning that you would be more generous if you could. It is comfortable to *have someone else as the "shit-minister."* If you really want to bring the family out of its trap and to help Sara out of her bind, you should let some shit stick to your wings. The whiteness and the beauty do not belong to you by a decree of nature. You two created these roles. When you avoid taking charge, you harm your wife and children. You are not really a white angel, for no angel can be a successful managing engineer. You play the white angel, and in that you are perhaps guilty of the greatest betrayal towards Sara: an ongoing, permanent betrayal, that keeps you blameless and leaves her black and in the lurch.*

The message had a strong effect upon the therapist. She began to see Sara and Abe in a different light. Sessions became limited to one hour and payment became prompt and regular.

Abe, struck by the final words of the message, started on a series of "self-defiling" projects. He told his eldest daughter that he had read her diary and found out about the stolen money. The daughter had to return the money to its place (which she managed to do without bringing the issue into the open). He got the children to perform household chores, while Sara slowly learned to accept and enjoy a more passive role.

Abe and Sara began meeting once a week at a fixed time to make plans or be together. Abe told Sara, for the first time, about his troubles with his boss. Sara supported him and helped him decide to look for a new job. The therapeutic sessions were devoted to planning how Abe could deepen his involvement in the household. Therapy was concluded three months after the critical intervention. A few months later Sara and Abe made a joint phone call to the therapist to tell her that Abe had found a new, prestigious job. He said proudly

---

*This was a well-known expression ("Scheissminister") in concentration camps, designating the person in charge of the latrines. Abe and Sara, second-generation Holocaust survivors, were sure to be affected by it.

that he had succeeded in keeping a good layer of shit over himself. Sara told the therapist that she thought no better of psychologists ("We religious people don't believe in that"), but that she was grateful for the help she (the therapist), as a human being, had given them.

CONCLUSION: A PLURALIST VIEW OF THE THERAPEUTIC RELATIONSHIP

Before the days of the pluralist revolution, each therapeutic school assumed that there was one right psychotherapeutic attitude, one ideal form of therapeutic relationship, and one way of handling problems in the relationship. For an experiential therapist, for instance, the right psychotherapeutic attitude was characterized by acceptance, genuineness, and warmth; the ideal form of therapeutic relationship by an I-Thou dialogue; the handling of relational problems by full transparency on the therapist's part. For an orthodox psychoanalyst, the right attitude was one of neutral, nonjudgmental listening; the ideal therapeutic relationship was the one that maximized transferential potential; relational problems were handled by transference interpretations. For a behavior therapist, the right attitude was scientific; the ideal relationship was that of teacher and pupil (or scientist and apprentice); problems in the relationship were addressed by precise definition of goals and clarification of means.

The pluralist revolution did away with the assumption that there is one royal way of therapeutic relating. Any contender to the title can, at times, be proved wrong. It is then necessary to examine the therapist's attitudes and reactions, and to change those that do not fit the case.

The pluralist approach echoes Alexander and French's concept of *the corrective emotional experience* (1946). A corrective experience would be created when the therapist assumed an attitude that was the absolute opposite of the one the patient had neurotically learned to expect on the basis of his or her upbringing. Thus, a patient whose parents had been excessively permissive would be best helped by a limiting therapist, and a patient whose parents had been strict and punitive would be best helped by a liberal and permissive one.* Any therapeutic attitude might thus prove wrong to a given patient, by reinforcing instead of refuting the dysfunctional expectations. Critical interventions could thus be viewed as creating a corrective emotional experience to the negative expectations that developed in the course of the therapy.

---

*This concept was much criticized when it was first proposed, in particular because it did away with the assumption of the one correct therapeutic attitude. At the time, the possibility of a plurality of attitudes smacked of charlatanism and manipulativeness.

6

THE UNIFYING FUNCTION

OF CRITICAL INTERVENTIONS

THERAPY, IN A PLURALIST AGE, is in constant danger of fragmentation (Cornsweet, 1983; Messer, 1986). It lacks the unifying glue provided by the concepts of a single theory and by the practices of a homogeneous school. In the schools' era, the therapist presented a clear image to the patient and the therapy was endowed with a sense of coherence. The patient was steadied by this meeting with a system of thought embodied in a congruent figure. Values, beliefs, and basic forms of relating were conveyed harmoniously. Compared to this, pluralist psychotherapy seems rather like an ever-shifting marketplace (Strenger & Omer, 1992).

Attempts have been made to remedy this situation by means of a *systematic eclecticism* (Beutler, 1986; Norcross, 1986) that proposes to make the therapy fit the patient according to a method well grounded upon either a meta-theory, a common psychotherapeutic language, or an unimpeachable body of fact. Unfortunately, the invisible worm of pluralism gnaws at the heart of metatheories, common languages, and what counts as acceptable fact, just as it did with the schools' theories, languages, and "facts." A replacement still waits to be found for the protective and stabilizing shell that was once supplied by unitary theory and school. As in biological evolution, a solution could perhaps be found by substituting the obsolete external skeleton of the theory or school with an internal one: an inner, steadying focus might pull together the forces that pull the therapy apart. A critical intervention provides such unifying focus.

THEMATIC UNITY

Establishing a focal theme is a crucial task in all varieties of short-term psychotherapy. When time is limited, a focus is needed to constrict and direct the flow of material. Without it, short-term therapy would do no more than touch upon the surface of its swarming issues. Treatment would become a table of contents.

The focal theme should be easy to remember and help to organize the patient's productions. These demands could be fulfilled by a vivid *life sketch* highlighting the role played by the symptoms in the patient's life journey. In formulating such a life sketch, the therapist says in one breath: "*This* is your problem and *this* is your life." If the formula proves auspicious, it takes hold in the patient's mind and binds to itself whatever transpires in the sessions. The modern drive for treatment briefness, together with the demands of the pluralist era for a new kind of therapeutic skeleton, have given rise to a variety of procedures for formulating life sketches (Omer, in press).

In its essence, the life sketch is not a novelty. Many of the pioneers of short-term psychotherapy were one-time psychoanalysts (Luborsky, 1984; Mann, 1973, 1981; Strupp & Binder, 1984), who used for their new task the tools with which they were familiar. The life sketch can thus be viewed, on the one hand, as a compressed version of the psychoanalytic case history and, on the other, as an expanded version of the classical interpretation. The demands of briefness, however, coupled with the skepticism of the post-schools' era, gave these old tools a new twist. In contrast to the old masters of the detailed and substantiated psychobiography, the life sketchers excel at the quick caricature, suggestive and striking rather than well-substantiated. The stress falls not on the portrayal's accuracy, but on its capacity to appeal, involve, provoke, and register in the mind. The life sketchers are not, as the masters of the old schools certainly were, personality theorists, presuming to unearth the foundations of human nature. They are not the Rembrandts but the Daumiers of psychotherapy, creating figures that by their very exaggeration and simplicity become almost emblematic of the characters they represent. In further distinction, the psychoanalytic life history emerges in full only by the end of treatment, whereas the life sketch is one of its opening events (Mann, 1973; Strupp & Binder, 1984). The traditional life history is not an intervention at all, but rather the resulting picture that validates the therapy's many interventions. The life sketch, in contrast, is the major intervention in short therapy, impelling it and directing its course.

Mann (1973, 1981) was the founding pioneer of the life-sketching tradition in short-term dynamic psychotherapy. His formula for the therapy's central issue achieves its feat of descriptive economy by means of three recurring elements: (a) an almost fixed opening ("You are a person that . . . " or "You have always . . . "); (b) a positive statement of the patient's strivings and achievements; and (c) an almost fixed ending describing the patient's chronic suffering as a clash between boundless strivings and bounded reality ("in spite of these achievements, however, you feel frustrated in that . . . "). For instance:

> You have always tried to fulfill an ideal of professional integrity and dedication, and you have had no little success as attested by your business achievements. However, you feel and have always felt an impostor about to be unmasked. (Mann, 1981, pp. 34–35)

When questioned by a skeptical professional audience on how such a life-embracing formula could be achieved in a single interview, Mann replied candidly that people's major strivings are not so diverse after all: some put love first; others, work; and still others, security. This answer shows how far the life sketch stands from a rigorous ideal of individualized portrayal. We are clearly within the boundaries of sympathetic caricature.

The drama of the life sketch as a clash between boundless striving and bounded reality sets the stage for the treatment, which is an unfolding of this basic dichotomy. The life sketch serves as a guiding beacon, evoking other experiences of striving and frustration. The strict twelve-session limit of Mann's therapy is a constant reminder of the boundless/bounded polarity, activating and checking the patient's longings for closeness. The life sketch is thus a preview of the whole therapy. It tells of the pity and the offense of harboring an infinity of yearning in a limited life and a restrictive reality.

Interpretations do play a subsidiary but peculiar role in this therapy, referring almost invariably to the basic experience depicted in the life sketch of wishing for more, more, endlessly more. It is as if a test were applied to each potential interpretation: "Does it fit with the central theme's message of finitude and boundedness?" If the answer is negative, the interpretation should be discarded. The life sketch thus becomes the touchstone for all other therapeutic interventions.

The critical messages described in this book are much indebted to Mann's central issue. In likeness to it, the critical message presents a life sketch that echoes the patient's desires, achievements, values and pains, and fulfills a guiding and unifying function in the therapy. The critical message, however, plays an additional role: it establishes a distinction between the new and the old therapy. It says (or implies): "*This*, not *that*, is the therapeutic problem; and *this*, not *that*, should be the therapy."

GOAL INTEGRATION

One particular variety of fragmentation that plagues psychotherapy in the pluralist era is the transiency of goals. Unballasted by a school, the therapist may easily be drawn into ever new pressing problems, and the treatment dissolve in a spray of shifting targets. When the changing goals are related—for instance, when it is just a matter of addressing different phobias or of switching from one interpersonal problem to another—therapy can bear the shifts and even be enriched by them. However, when the goals demand different and sometimes conflicting approaches, the pluralist therapist becomes perplexed. The typical dilemma of this kind is choosing between symptomatic and personal goals.

A rough division can be drawn in psychotherapy between two broad classes of approaches: the directive/behavioral and the nondirective/psychodynamic/experiential (London, 1986). The first is the class of *symptom-oriented*, the second of *person-oriented* therapies. A symptom-oriented therapy defines its goals in observable and circumscribed terms. A person-oriented therapy defines them in the terms of developmental tasks (Budman & Gurman, 1988). The symptom-oriented therapy deals with targets, skills, and concrete achievements; the person-oriented therapy, with growth, transformation, and release.

The choice between a symptomatic and a personal focus is often viewed as mutually exclusive: one must level one's efforts either at symptom modification or at inner change. The single-minded person-oriented therapist believes that personal development is the royal way to symptomatic change; the contrary is true for the symptom-oriented therapist. No real choice is therefore involved for therapists who dwell secure in a stable orientation. For the pluralist, however, the choice can be paralyzing. A critical intervention supplying an *integrative focus*, which coordinates symptomatic and personal goals in a reciprocal mutuality, might then bring release from this dilemma (Omer, 1993a).

The integrative focus is a formula that gives equal weight to the symptomatic and the personal focuses, establishing between them a causal mutuality: progress in one entails progress in the other. The formula has two parts: the first provides a rationale linking the two focuses, and the second renders their symmetrical relationship explicit. For instance (the two parts of the integrative focus are initialed as "a" and "b"):

(1) A young woman, whose grandparents on both sides were Holocaust survivors, had been reared in the belief that only excellence leads to survival. Any sign of imperfection on her part would meet with angry rejection, particularly from her father. Later in life, when faced with the need to perform, she would panic and blame others. She was given the following integrative message: (a) You learned from your father that rejection is the price of imperfection. Today, in your performance anxiety and your blaming behavior, you keep alive within yourself your bad relationship with him. (b) Your relationship with your father and your anxious and blaming reactions are thus two sides of the same problem. As you learn not to panic or blame others, you will grow free from your father's dominance. And as you understand that you are no longer your father's frightened little girl, you will become able to cope with potential failure.

(2) A 17-year-old girl was sent to the school psychologist because she was often found doped or drunk. She showed little interest in talking about these problems, but spoke willingly about her confusion on personal and sexual matters: she was an adopted child and felt attracted to women. The therapist, however, could not be content with a personal focus alone, for any progress in the personal area would be countered by drugs, booze, and the social ties they involved. The following integra-

tive message was therefore formulated: (a) You feel deeply mixed up about your identity: you don't know who your parents were, you are sexually confused and you don't know what you want. Whenever you start to discern a personal line, a pale thread linking your wishes, feelings, and acts, you erase it by getting high or drunk. Drugs and alcohol work on you like sandstorms covering up the traces of your burgeoning identity. On the other hand, not knowing who you are, you are drawn to drugs to replenish your inner void. (b) The two problems are actually one: in keeping away from drugs and alcohol, you will gradually discern signs of personal continuity and find out what your inner feelings and wishes are. And as you learn to know what you want and who you are, it will become easier to keep away from drugs and alcohol.*

In developing an integrative focus, the therapist is not just allowed but *required* to consider both a symptomatic and a personal perspective. As a mutually supportive relationship between the two goals is established, the integrative focus converts the conceptual seesaw into a source of power. Each goal is made to imply the other, symptomatic work becoming charged with personal overtones, and personal work with symptomatic ones. The integrative focus thus offers a grasp on both the personal and the symptomatic motivational handles, leading to a therapy with higher levels of commitment.

The formula helps the perplexed therapist in a variety of ways: (1) it relates disparate therapeutic interventions to a common theme; (2) it creates a wide conceptual net to make sense of new material; (3) it liberates the therapist from a paralyzing choice; and (4) it enhances the therapist's sense of efficacy, to the benefit of the therapeutic alliance. Let us examine a detailed example.

---

*In case 5 and in the final intervention of case 14 there are additional examples of integrative foci.

Case 15: The Philandering Politician

Shlomo, a politician very active in orthodox Jewish circles, came to therapy with a complaint of compulsive infidelity. He had had dozens of extramarital affairs, almost all characterized by low levels of personal involvement. He had twice become involved in long-term affairs, the last one still active at the time he applied for therapy. He asked for help against his urge, which not only conflicted deeply with his religious beliefs and way of life but also endangered his family, career, and public standing. In particular, he wanted to put an end to his two-year involvement with a woman who was in love with him and had expectations that he would eventually divorce his wife and marry her. He found it extremely hard to disappoint or set boundaries with his woman friends. In spite of disliking his wife acutely, divorce was not an option, because of his social position. Spaced-out and rather perfunctory sexual contacts (which he initiated to prevent suspicion) were the only sort of intimacy he experienced with her.

Shlomo's philandering urge stemmed from a variety of sources. He had matured early sexually and had masturbated (a sin much worse than philandering for a religious Jew) from his early teens, arguing with God that He should not have given him such desire without the means of withstanding it. In spite of these arguments, he suffered greatly from guilt feelings and fears of punishment. Another source of his urge was Shlomo's burning curiosity about the world outside the orthodox pale. His sexual partners were all nonreligious women, and he enjoyed partaking of their lives and experiences. The strongest source of all, however, seemed to be Shlomo's insatiable need for admiration. To be told, as he often was, that he was "the manliest" and "the best of them all" brought him celestial bliss. The glimmer of appreciation in a woman's eyes was his highest reward.

He had been the pampered only son of a family of well-to-do merchants. He was called "the little prince"; childhood pictures of him dressed up as a small grandee lent credence to the epithet. Shlomo's fall from this princely position was sudden: at the age of 12, he was sent into a yeshiva, to live and study with scores of other children. When he came home for visits, things were no longer the same: the paradise of parental worship had given way to a prosaic attitude towards him. Although, thanks to his brilliant intellect, he reached an eminent position in his new environment, Shlomo was left yearning for what he had lost.

He developed an unslakeable thirst for esteem. He always had to be unique and incomparable. Intellectual and sexual admiration served equally as fuels for this need. An episode from his current life illustrated how, in his mental economy, one form of esteem could be exchanged for another: he usually had the honor of commenting weekly on the Bible in his community synagogue. When, for once, the heads of the community invited a visiting guest's commentary instead, Shlomo protested by staying home and taking revenge (on God?) by surreptitiously phoning (on a Sabbath!) one of his most admiring woman friends and asking her for a tryst. The appreciation deficit incurred by his snubbing at the synagogue was thus to be recouped by a dose of womanly regard.

Therapy had followed two rather independent lines. The first was problem-focused: the therapist acceded to Shlomo's request to help him set limits to his affair. Shlomo's need to please had led to his lover's becoming ever more demanding: she phoned him constantly at his office, asked for daily trysts, and made plans for weekends together and a holiday abroad. Shlomo did not dare contradict her. With the therapist's support, he made it clear to her, for the first time, that he was not going to divorce his wife. She reacted by breaking off the relationship, but soon she renewed it on less demanding terms. Even then, however, the affair was dangerous and scandal lurked around the corner. After two anonymous telephone calls to his wife, Shlomo declared to the therapist his determined intention to end the affair. But still, he abstained from acting. The therapist, apparently more frightened than Shlomo, found himself trapped in the unrewarding role of Jimminy Cricket.

The second therapeutic line was personal, focusing on the sources of Shlomo's need for admiration. Shlomo reacted well to the explorative therapy: he was emotionally involved, contributed significant material, and found the dialogue with the therapist rewarding. The therapist, however, was greatly concerned because after a year of therapy there seemed to be no carryover from the personal exploration into the symptomatic area. Worried about the danger of a public scandal, the therapist brought the case for consultation.

At the beginning, the group inclined toward the explorative line. The problem-oriented strategy had led to a negative complementarity, as Shlomo's unconcern about the brewing storm grew with the therapist's concern. No therapeutic shortcut seemed available: treatment would have to deal in depth with Shlomo's lack of an "inner admiring eye." The therapist, however, kept coming back to realities: Shlomo's career and family might be shattered before the very first laps of the therapeutic journey had been covered. The long-term personal plan would leave the therapist without a client or with the shreds of one. The group then veered to the other pole, starting on a search for rescue strategies. Not for long, however. Shlomo's apparent lack of an autonomous sense of self made all practical options seem trite. Thus, each therapeutic line seemed compelling on its own, but it was impossible to stick to it for more than a short while. The following integrative focus was formulated as a possible answer to this unproductive wavering:

Since early adolescence, you suffered horrible pangs of conscience, because of your powerful sexual drive. Today, however, you are the slave of another, more tyrannous, urge: you are addicted to the admiration of your woman partners. Like a drug addict or an alcoholic, you've developed a craving for the sign of appreciation, the expression of enjoyment, the grateful stroke. Like an addict, you ask me to set brakes upon you, to help you control what you feel to be beyond your control. No good, however, comes to an addict from another person's assuming responsibility. I was wrong to try to stop you. I cannot be your rescuer, and my trying will cause you damage.

You need external admiration so much because you lack an inner admiring voice. We have started to understand how this lack could have come about. Getting to know this better, getting closer to the sense of loss that you experienced as a child and learning to listen to your inner glimmerings of self-respect is one of your life tasks. Learning not to give in to your urge is another—more practical and no less vital—for if you fail in it, your family life and your career may be shattered. The two goals are deeply related: each time you withstand your urge and refuse the easy path to external admiration, you will become better able to respect yourself and recognize your inner admiring voice. And as you become more connected to that voice and understand how you came to lose track of it, you will be better able to withstand temptation.

The influence of this unifying message on the therapy was complex. It pulled together the two strands that had been previously pursued separately. The therapist, furthermore, gave up the role of Shlomo's keeper. Shlomo became serious in his efforts to stop the affair and, after a few unsuccessful attempts, asked the therapist for help in managing the separation. The therapist acquiesced conditionally: it should be clear that the therapist's help was undertaken at Shlomo's request and on his responsibility; furthermore, the therapist would cease helping immediately if Shlomo tried to shirk any commitment he assumed. A behavioral "weaning" program was then instituted and pursued to a successful end. The addiction metaphor, however, was not invariably helpful: after the separation, Shlomo used it as an excuse for his other sexual misdemeanors. This brought therapy into a new phase, characterized by an existential dialogue on the issue of Shlomo's evasion of personal responsibility and his paradoxical religiosity.

CONCLUSION: THE UNIFYING DRIVE
IN PLURALIST PSYCHOTHERAPY

Soon after discovering diversity, psychotherapists felt a thirst for unity. Norcross (1990) has counted over fifty models of psychotherapy integration aiming at a synthesis of theories, techniques, and formats. Curiously, however, this multiplicity of schemes for integration seems not to bother their proponents. On the contrary, the integrationists seem to be the very ones who keep warning against premature attempts at an overall integrative framework. Thus, they seem to hold to and let go of their models at the same time. How can we understand this apparent paradox?

One must be a pluralist to become an integrationist. Without an awareness of the limitations of absolute formulations and of the legitimacy of different approaches, there is no need to integrate. On the other hand, the infinite variety of modern psychotherapy is quite disorienting. The era that began with a feeling that a thousand flowers shall bloom led soon to overwhelming dizziness. Variety and chaos are close neighbors. Therapists seek an antidote to this threat in the establishment of communication: if we can talk to and understand each other, translate our insights into one another's language, develop common projects, reach a local consensus, we are no longer totally at loss, not completely alone, not irremediably unjustified. The integrative activity is thus pursued for itself, no less than for its results.

The give-and-take of consultation belongs to this new tradition: therapists from different orientations meet together to help a colleague out of a theoretical and practical dead-end. It takes courage to abandon a well-practiced therapeutic attitude and perspective with which the therapist feels comfortable. The motivation to do so comes from two sources: the sense of impasse and confusion, and the hope for productive dialogue with a community of peers. Until now, we have focused on the critical message, which is the product of the consultation session. Its process, to which we now turn, is no less important.

7

THE PROCESS
OF CONSULTATION

THE CONSULTATION STARTS with an impasse and ends with an intervention. The therapist begins by an exposition about the patient and the therapy, while the consultant and the group try to clarify the impasse with questions about the therapeutic narrative, strategy, and interaction. In the beginning, the group typically shares and reflects the therapist's reactions: a critical response to the therapist's exposition is quite rare. At times, the presentation is so cogent that the group feels as paralyzed as the therapist. After the exposition, the group tries to grapple with the apparent hopelessness of the case. The very sense of paralysis may be of help in discerning what in the case's conceptualization and management seems most conducive to the impasse. By focusing on what arouses the greatest pessimism, one may get an inkling of a new perspective. For instance, a patient can be described as irremediably aggressive, sick, or inhuman; a family as cruel, crazy, or engulfing. These black attributes nullify all options and allow for no hope. The consul-

128

tant may then pinpoint the negative formulation, saying, for instance: "So long as we think of the patient only as x, y, and z, we cannot be of help." Gradually, what had seemed like a solid flaw rooted in the patient's very nature is perceived anew as resulting from an inappropriate narrative, a bad strategy, an interactional bind. New possible descriptions, tactics, and reactions begin to surface—sometimes in orderly fashion, more often in a jumble. Out of the apparent confusion, some of the new ideas begin to coalesce, sometimes catalyzed by a felicitous expression or image.

The consultant may then ask the group to formulate a tentative intervention or offer one himself. Group members criticize the proposal and suggest improvements. The therapist, however, remains as the final judge of the message's fit to the patient and the therapy under discussion. After all, he or she will have to deliver the intervention and be most responsible for its consequences.

As the intervention is gradually honed and polished, therapist, group, and consultant talk more and more in one voice. The consultative work seems finished. The group's function, however, is still not exhausted: since the group backs the therapist in delivering the intervention, the therapist feels bound to report to the group on its results. If necessary, the group discusses the case again and, occasionally, a new intervention is formulated to strengthen the first, undo its damage, or address a new impasse.

A similar process of consultation, which begins from a paralyzing perspective, is followed by an attempt to stir up maximum diversity, and ends with the collapse of this diversity into a new, unifying formula, characterizes the work of the Milan group of family therapy (Boscolo et al., 1987). The Milan approach regards family problems as due to limiting narratives that involve family members in mutually restrictive and damaging interactions. The task of the consulting team is to open the way for new narratives and interactions.

The consultation proper is preceded by a family interview conducted by one of the consultants, while the others usually attend behind a one-way screen. The interview clarifies the narrative in which the family (and often also the therapist who invited the consultants) is stuck. The first aim of the team discussion is to induce a plurality of narratives and perspectives. To foster diversity, the discussants may be forbidden to express agreement with each other, or enjoined to hold different family members as responsible for the problem ("You blame it all on the father, you on the mother, and I on the son"), or asked to follow each other's comments with something completely disconnected ("I feel the mother is most despondent." "And I think the elder son makes too much money for this family." "Sure, but the father hates the therapist."). Gradually, the disparate comments and perspectives are woven into one systemic hypothesis that is embodied in a message to be read to the family. The appropriate integrative level has been reached when the team experiences "a systemic orgasm" (presumably, the exhilarating experience of transcending the limited individual hypotheses). When this accord is reached, the consultant who conducted the interview returns to the family with the message.

The parallels between the Milan consultation and the present one go beyond the procedural level. Both arose from a disbelief in unitary theories and normative models of individual and family functioning. Both assume that narratives, interactions, and strategies are closely interlinked and that stalemate at one level feeds stalemate at others. Both emphasize the value of integrative formulations that pull together a variety of perspectives. Both strive to give the perplexed, anchorless therapist a backing in the group's consensus. Both are true children of the pluralist era.

The next example consists of a transcript of a consultation session.* Th stands for therapist, Co, for consultant (myself), M1, M2, M3, M4, M5, and M6, for group members. Comments on the consultation process are printed in italics.

Case 16: A Family Tradition of Infidelity

TH: My involvement in this case began with the wife, Shira. The husband, Efi, joined later. Shira came to therapy when she found out that Efi was having an affair. She was very depressed and couldn't decide what to do. She is 40 years old and works as a manager in a department store. Efi works in a family business with his father and brother. They have been married for 17 years and have three children. Efi didn't want to come to therapy or talk about the affair. Shira described herself as a soccer ball and Efi as a player who sits on the bench and doesn't even kick the ball.

CO: Does she want to be kicked?

TH: That's the irony of the image. When I asked her what had to happen so that something would change, she answered: "I have to be turned into a doormat. If I found out that Efi went on with the affair, then perhaps I would do something." Officially, Efi broke off the affair when Shira caught him, but there are signs that it is still going on. For instance, almost every morning the telephone rings once. Shira thinks this may be an agreed sign between Efi and his lover that she is alone at home. The affair started in a folk-dancing class. In that very same class, Efi's brother had also begun an affair a few months before. The brother, too, went through a period of doubting whether to stay in his marriage or not. He even left home for a while and went to live with his lover, but after a couple of months he came back. He went

---

*I have made minor changes in the tape-recorded text so as to improve grammar and reduce repetition.

to individual therapy and has apparently overcome his personal crisis. He even took his wife for a reconciliation tour in Europe. Efi also thought about leaving but couldn't bring himself to it. When he thought about leaving, he had a panic attack and was sure he was going to die. He remained at home, but avoided all contact with Shira. No touching, no talking. As for his brother, Efi completely discounts the reconciliation. He says it is only a show.

M1: Do Efi and his wife sleep separately?

TH: They sleep in the same room, but since the affair began Efi has never had sex with Shira. Before the affair, Shira had been cold and detached. Her mother had always been very loving and dedicated to other people, but not to her family. This pattern of detachment became Shira's, too. She could hardly express warmth, even to her children. Efi was very attracted to her, but she felt quite cold. Sex was very low in her priorities; orgasms, she had once in a year maybe. All in all, he had always desired her and she had rebuffed him. Today, she says that he is totally indifferent to her. She feels like a carcass, a "cold chunk of meat" for him.

CO: How did the individual sessions go?

TH: We had about eight individual sessions. She wanted to become able to express herself, to show more involvement and warmth. With the children it worked very well, but when she tried it with Efi, nothing came of it. He simply didn't respond. We also worked at developing her friendships and family links outside the home. She became more assertive at work and got herself a better position. After a while, I phoned Efi and he agreed to come. He is an extremely anxious person. He visits a therapist who helps him with the panic attacks. I talked to this therapist, with Efi's consent, and he told me that Efi refuses to deal with the marital issue, asking only for symptomatic help with the panic attacks. When he has no panic attacks for two weeks in a row, he stops coming. The therapist helped to convince

Efi to come and see me and, eventually, to begin marital therapy.

M2: The panic attacks started with the marital crisis?

TH: He had had panic attacks before, but during the affair, whenever he thought about leaving home, he would get a panic attack which "forced" him to stay. There is a family pattern in this story: when he was 15, he found out that his father was having an affair with a distant relative. His father chose not to end the marriage and the affair was officially terminated. In Efi's opinion, however, something is still alive between the two, at least on an emotional level. When Efi's affair became known, his son was also 15, the same age he was when he found out about his father's affair. Efi's brother was 17 at the time of their father's affair, and the brother's son was also 17 at the time his (the brother's) affair exploded.

CO: The story is so good that it would be a pity to spoil it.

The therapist's exposition has disclosed a rigid element in the family's self-limiting narrative: a fixed pattern of extramarital affairs, any apparent deviation from which is discounted as unreal or only a show. The following passage illustrates how such a narrative may acquire the power of unavoidable fate.

TH: The father was adamantly opposed to either of the sons' leaving their wives. The brother tried but failed. When I asked him to describe his brother's present relationship with his wife, Efi said that nothing had "really" changed. "Why," he asked, "do you think that there is any real thing between them? He only plays at talking, going to the movies or going to bed with her. His heart is not in it." As for Shira, Efi's heart is definitely not in it. He does not want her to suffer, but he feels nothing for her, not even anger. For him, she is only so much air.

M2: So why does he stay?

TH: Efi is very dependent on his father. He feels he cannot oppose him. Furthermore, all three of them, Efi, his father, and his brother, are partners in the business. A family fight might shatter the family living.

M3: Such dependence is typical in family businesses. I know of two couples who have been living like that for forty years, destroying each other but chained together by the business. Everything is linked together, like in a beehive: the nuclear family with the extended family, personal problems with business problems. You simply cannot break away.

This comment illustrates how the feeling of paralysis begins to contaminate the group. The problem is now seen as transcending this particular couple and has become the unchangeable condition of people involved in family businesses.

M4: How does Shira react to the family's involvement in the story?

TH: Her behavior is very different from that of her sister-in-law. When the affair with the in-laws exploded, the wife broke down, threatened suicide, and ran to everybody in the family crying for help. Shira did nothing like that. She kept it all to herself. Efi's father, however, went into action anyhow. He told Efi that he would never forgive him if he left Shira and the children.

CO: How did the therapeutic dialogue with Efi develop?

The exposition still has not clarified the therapeutic strategy and relationship. Particularly in a story with so many juicy ramifications, the discussion may tend to center on the patients and the family, leaving the therapy in the shadow. The consultation might then become limited to a reinterpretation of the patients' personal and family dynamics. The consultant steps in to correct this tendency.

Tʜ: He came for two individual sessions and was very coopera-
tive. We then started having sessions together with Shira.
He speaks his mind and expresses his feelings. But he gets
extremely anxious before the sessions. By the time he arrives he seems completely run down by the anxiety. What
happens at home, however, seems to be just the opposite of
what happens in the sessions. When we have a difficult
session, talking about divorce, Efi becomes more pleasant
and friendly at home. He may watch TV with Shira or speak
a little. He even bought a bracelet for her birthday, but
asked the children to give it to her. When we have a more
positive session, Efi becomes silent and unapproachable at
home. It seems as if he were bent on keeping a fixed distance between himself and Shira, compensating for whatever happens in the session.

*The complementarity of the therapeutic interaction is de-
scribed here with the strictness of a mathematical equation.
Whenever the therapist brings about a rapprochement in the
session, the couple reacts by becoming more detached at home,
and vice versa.*

M1: Maybe it would be better to assume a different stance in
the therapy. Instead of working at improving the marriage
it might be better to talk more about divorce. This might
work paradoxically.
Tʜ: When I saw that the constructive talks were rebounding,
I tried to convince them to go to a lawyer, at least to get an
opinion on the problem of the family business and how their
rights of ownership could be divided. They followed my
advice and the atmosphere at home improved. This is what
I meant by that feeling of a fixed marital distance. Efi's lover
also got the opposite reaction from the one she intended.
When she pushed hard to get Efi to leave home, Efi got

more panic attacks and it became clear that he would not leave. Shira tried to get closer and help him, and he rebuffed her. Everything boomerangs with him.

The therapist has been induced into the marital seesaw, alternating between a strategy of rapprochement and a strategy of distancing (examining the divorce option). Like them, she swings between the poles of together and apart. Each step in any direction is followed by untoward responses which lead to a retreat into the opposite one.

M5: Did she try to have sex with him?

TH: She tried to seduce him a few times. She threw hints, dressed provocatively, but — nothing. He said that in the past this would have driven him wild, but now it leaves him cold. This is the situation. This is where they are, and this is where I am stuck. No matter what I do, they won't budge. What can I do with them?

This quasi-formal declaration of impasse signals the end of the exposition. From this point on the group becomes more active, raising new strategies and perspectives.

M2: What keeps him from leaving? What is it that he cannot separate from?

TH: I think he is scared stiff of the very possibility of change. And she is paralyzed too. With each new rebuff on Efi's part, she becomes more hurt and more restless, but does nothing.

CO: Does she yearn for intimacy with him?

TH: Today, after so many rejections she is full of anger. Underneath, however, she needs closeness and is happiest when Efi becomes more affable. But somehow, the situation is kept just as it is. Each step forwards leads to a step backwards.

M2: Does he want to love her again?

TH: He doesn't know. He sits on the fence.

CO: I once treated the lover of such a husband. For ten years the husband kept both lover and wife in a state of utter uncertainty. In the end he left the lover, divorced the wife, and married a third woman, all in two months.

The sense of paralysis brings associations of similar cases, endlessly stuck in the same bind. The group members, including myself, are steeped in the narrative's sense of inevitability. It is as if we were nodding our heads and saying to ourselves: "We all know these never-ending stories." Many consultations pass through such a stage: it is the emotional marker of the closed narrative.

TH: I asked him what makes him come to therapy. He said he doesn't know. He is afraid of hurting others. He feels almost physically immobilized.

M1: I don't feel there is any real positive feeling between them today. Only fear keeps them together: fear for the children, fear of the father, fear for the business, and blah-blah-blah. It is clear that taking a positive therapeutic stand of trying to improve the marriage leads nowhere.

TH: Right. That's why I started to work on the readiness to separate.

M1: Maybe it would be best to stick to this work of separation. This could be more productive, at least tactically. The dominant factor now is the fear of being alone. You could inoculate them against that.

CO: How?

M1: For instance, by telling her to rehearse her life alone in fantasy. Telling her to pay attention to her feelings and watch how the initial anxiety will gradually subside and pave the way for other feelings. She can be given a daily parting ritual, like saying "Goodbye" in her heart. Saying "Goodbye" to Efi's presence at home, to their meals together, to his touch, to his voice. Whenever he talks to her, she should say "Goodbye" and add to herself: "This may be the last time." Anything good that happens should be taken as a farewell. And anything bad, too. All along she should pay attention to her feelings, to the sadness, to the anxiety, to the anger, but also to the hope and the readiness for something different.

TH: That's why I referred them to a lawyer. I wanted the divorce option to be less frightening and therefore less paralyzing. They reacted well to the meeting with the lawyer. It showed them that the practical difficulties were not insuperable and they became less frightened and more relaxed. But then, Efi's father reappeared and occupied the center of the stage. He is overpowering, as far as Efi is concerned. I once asked Efi what his father would say if he sat in the treatment room and listened to Efi's thoughts and feelings. Efi answered: "He would never let me leave."

The exchange between M1 and Th illustrates the inductive power of ineffective strategies. M1 suggests a new avenue, clearly different from what the therapist had attempted before. The therapist, however, responds by assimilating the new idea to something she had already tried without success. Therapists are similar, in this respect, to ineffective parents who respond to any suggestion on how to manage their children with the remark: "Oh, we have tried that already!" In the process of group discussion such new ideas rise and fall. They may, however, be picked up again if they fit with an alternative narrative and a new view of the therapeutic relationship.

M2: Does Efi fear his father's responses more than Shira's or this other woman's?

TH: He is very dependent and the father is very powerful. The brother, who is supposed to be stronger than Efi, tried to be independent, but failed and had to crawl back to the fold. For Efi this is proof enough that leaving is impossible.

M4: I get the feeling that this man is no longer alive.

TH: I agree, and he thinks so too. He talks about himself as living a lingering death.

This death image is very common. Describing a patient as "emotionally dead" often serves a self-justifying purpose in a stuck treatment, for therapists cannot be expected to resuscitate the dead. If unchallenged, the death metaphor reinforces the sense of therapeutic helplessness and threatens to turn the consultation into a commiseration session.

M5: Nothing interests him?

TH: He works hard. He is also active in sports. He plays basketball and goes to the gym. He is very athletic.

M4: You can trust a hypochondriac to keep fit.

This interchange illustrates the pull of the death metaphor, even in the face of contradictory evidence. Being active in sports, playing basketball, and frequenting the gym are rather strenuous activities for a corpse. The physical activity is easily discounted, however, by being ascribed to Efi's hypochondria.

M5: Was there anything else that interested him before?

TH: When he looks back over his previous life, he feels that the real high point was the affair. Up to then, he felt quite dead.

M2: He was much attracted to his wife, however.

M1: How was he with the children?

TH: I think he was a good father. Even now, he doesn't neglect the children. I think he gave a lot to the family, but received little.

CO: I don't think that's true. He received a lot, but not all he wanted and not in the way he wanted. If we forget this, we will tend to see the marriage as dead from the beginning and thus doom it for the future. He was much alive in the marriage. I wouldn't say a man is "dead" when he feels as sexy as he did about Shira.

TH: That's true. Even today he fantasizes a lot about his lover.

By focusing on Efi's previous feelings for Shira, his involvement with the children, his sexual desire and fantasy life, the group gradually succeeded in resuscitating him. The death metaphor was thus kept at bay.

CO: Does he fantasize about living with her?

TH: Very much. He misses their meetings, their talks, and everything he lacked before. But he won't take the jump. His parents had the same kind of relationship. His mother was very similar to Shira. Cold and distant.

M2: Does he criticize Shira as a mother, too?

TH: No.

M2: But you feel that she lacks something as a mother.

TH: Yes, and so does she. We worked at it and she became more aware of her detached attitude and she is changing for the better.

CO: Did you plan to go on working toward making divorce a concrete option?

TH: I wonder. I tried this because what I had tried before wasn't leading anywhere.

CO: What had you tried before?

TH: I tried to bring the marriage into working order—for instance, by improving the communication between them. There were some results: Efi opened up as he had never dared before. He talked openly about the rebuffs he had suffered from Shira. They would start talking and the session would grow alive. But then, in the next session they would tell me that, at home, the coldness became even more pronounced.

M5: I get the impression that intimacy is a big problem. He grew up in a family with no intimacy. His mother was cold and detached and his father was emotionally involved outside the marriage. Also in this marriage, there was a lot of detachment. Even the affair has more fantasy than real intimacy to it. I think the therapy should focus on this intimacy problem.

TH: With the couple?

M5: Maybe with him.

TH: I thought so too, and so did his other therapist. But he is not willing to work on this issue. He keeps canceling his sessions with the other therapist and comes only when he has a panic attack.

M3: Does he think that the marriage is hopeless?

TH: He doesn't see any possibility of action. He says that only time, a lot of time, will perhaps bring a change.

M6: They seem to be fighting against a family curse. The curse was there in the previous generation and perhaps even before that, dooming all marriages in the family. You can raise the issue of the curse, give it a name, and explore how they keep the curse alive.

M2: Yes, then one could externalize the curse and turn it into the family enemy, in the Michael White* tradition.

M5: Shira also fulfills a role in the curse. She takes upon herself the role of the mother and becomes cold and detached. Shira's mother was similar to Efi's, and this allows her to play her part well.

TH: Yes, this description fits well with what went on with the parents. Efi's and Shira's mutual choice was not arbitrary.

---

*"Externalizing the problem" is a strategy for dealing with closed narratives well-known to family therapists (White & Epston, 1990).

M5: Both perform roles that were forced upon them by the curse.

M4: What was the initial source of their attraction to each other? We might perhaps link this to the motif of the curse.

TH: He is basically a warm person who invested a lot in the family and the rearing of the children. These are the qualities that she found in him. As for her, she is very attractive and sort of aristocratic. He feels this nobility in her, even today. In a way, we might even say that he was attracted by her apparent coldness.

The "family curse" captivated the group's attention and offered a way out of the prevailing pessimism. Such a metaphor, particularly when couched in a felicitous expression, may fulfill a catalyzing function in the consultation and in the therapy. The image of the curse opened up the closed narrative. As an additional character to the family cast, it unbalanced the stalemated view of the marital interaction. The group elaborated on the metaphor, examining, in its light, the couple's mutual choice: Efi had looked for someone who reminded him of his mother, but in a positive way. Shira fulfilled this role by her very detachment, which was positively connoted as an aristocratic sign.

M4: What did he miss in his family of origin, that he thought he might find in Shira?

TH: I don't know (pause). The family exerted a strong pull. Everyone was involved with everyone else and in the business. She raised his hopes for independence. Because of her, he tried to become financially autonomous. They moved for a while to another town and Efi tried a new job, but it didn't work. He sort of blames her for coming back, though the decision wasn't hers. He feels that she disappointed him in his hopes for independence. But, I feel some difficulty with the idea of the family curse. I don't think he is ready to work on the marriage at all. He is still stuck in his extramarital fantasies.

In this excerpt, the therapist opens up a new interpretive line on the issue of Efi's frustrated wish for independence. This new line is cut short, however, by the realities of the case, as she understands them: Efi will not respond positively to the new line or to the curse metaphor, because he is still not ready to work on the marriage. This mutual feedback between therapist and group is crucial in making the intervention fit the therapist and the patient. The new line is not neglected, as can be seen in what follows, but a way must be found to handle the difficulty. The therapist must be satisfied for the intervention to take hold.

Co: It seems that, for him, working on the marriage is a betrayal of his lover.

Th: Precisely. He isn't ready yet. If he gets closer to his wife he betrays his lover.

M6: Maybe this is part of the curse.

M3: Yes, he has this tendency to live always with something that cannot be attained.

M6: The tendency in the family is to solve problems by looking out of the marriage. This is part of the curse. The tendency is to blame the spouse and stay loyal to someone outside.

M3: For me the family curse is that at a certain stage in life, something dies within you.

M4: I think it is very important that he hoped to become able to separate from the family through his wife. This points to a real need of his, something he yearns for. But, if he failed in this, and failed in his attempt to grow alive with his lover, he is really dead.

When the curse metaphor gets into trouble, the death meta-phor raises its head. An attempt was made by M3 to fuse the two metaphors into one, describing the family curse as a tendency for early emotional death. The new narrative, how-ever, cannot offer an alternative to the old one if it is absorbed by it.

M4: Maybe we could bring the marriage issue to the fore by "spoiling" the affair.*

TH: I tried that too, but it failed.

CO: We are thinking about technique but we still haven't a good conceptualization of the case.

M4: I thought that if the wife has once signaled the way to-wards separation-individuation, we could pursue that direc-tion again.

CO: The idea of the curse or any kind of direct marital work are still premature, for Efi is still not sure that he wants to salvage the marriage. When he makes a step in one direction he gets scared and goes back to the other. He cannot work on the marriage or leave it, and the therapist cannot help them stay together or separate. Before getting to the family curse, we have to stop this shilly-shallying. I have a strategic principle for dealing with mutually canceling goals: "Choose a therapeutic course that advances both." We could say something like this: "You've accumulated lots of anger in the marriage. The anger now blocks the way: you cannot improve the marriage and you cannot separate. When one tries to separate with so much anger, one feels terribly fright-ened, for the anger makes everything so explosive. We have to deal with the anger so that you may become able either to separate or to improve the marriage."

---

*To "spoil" the affair means to introduce comments and hints that bring about a deterioration of the romance.

The attempt to develop a new narrative seemed promising, but the therapist still felt that the road was blocked on account of the negative complementarity that nullified all attempts in a clear direction. My suggestion was to define a new goal which might free Efi from the need for immediate choice.

TH: The problem is that we don't see the anger. Efi is apathetic rather than angry. He doesn't want to hurt her.

CO: Let us correct the message, then: "It is not that you are both seething with hatred, obsessing all along about revenge. Your anger is different: it stems from deep hurts accumulated over a long time. You, Efi, tried to get closer to Shira for years and years, and were rejected again and again. You courted her, desired her, yearned for her, loved her, and were rebuffed in return. Huge stores of silent frustration built up inside you, until you couldn't bear it any longer. From then on, it was you, Shira, who became the butt of endless rejection. You were turned into a nonperson, you were not even kicked about, you were not even used as a doormat. You became invisible, you became a ghost. No wonder that you two cannot separate or work at improving the marriage. This is the sure recipe for the most destructive of divorce proceedings, for when people try to divorce without being able really to separate, they must tear themselves and each other apart. No wonder, Efi, that you are afraid of a heart attack. People die in such circumstances. It is impossible to separate without communicating, without a common ground. Two things must happen so that you may either become able to separate or to work on the marriage: you must become able to talk, to communicate, to develop some semblance of a normal life; and you both must get stronger individually, developing your own resources and anchors. You Shira, must see yourself as a person, cultivate friendships, personal goals and interests. You Efi, must become more independent from your family, espe-

cially from your father. Only by doing these things will you
become able either to come together or to separate."

M6: I think this won't work. There is something fishy in the
idea of getting closer in order to separate.

M4: Maybe we should find an additional reason for the need
to work at the anger. They have to work at the anger and
the hurt because anger and hurt get people stuck. They
won't be able to go on with their lives without dealing with
the hurt.

*The group refuses to accept an intervention that fails to
meet the complexities of the case. Pluralism does not imply
that "anything goes" and that any therapeutic yarn would do.
On the contrary, lacking an absolute basis for justifying a therapeutic course, therapist, consultant, and group must strive for
a local consensus, without which the therapist will lack the
backing for the required changes.*

CO: Well, let's try again: "With such anger and such pain, it is
not only that you cannot make a decision about the marriage. You cannot go on with your lives. You have to deal
with these hurts, to acknowledge them, to confess them, to
make and receive reparation. Otherwise you cannot go on.
That's what we should do in the therapy."

M4: Working at the anger and the hurts is the only way to
avoid falling again into the same trap. So that in the future,
if he develops a new relationship, with his wife or with someone else, he may become inoculated against the curse.

CO: Let's go back to the objection that it won't be convincing
to say to them that they have to get closer to become able
to separate. Maybe we could say something like this: "Before
you decide on separating or staying together, you have to
know the hurts, those that you have inflicted and those that
you have received. Otherwise you won't be able to build a
new relationship, either with each other or with anybody

else. You have to unblock the way to a better marriage or to any future relationship by acknowledging the hurts, and by making and receiving reparation."

M4: I think it's too early to talk of reparation. You may lose your strategic leverage, for Efi is still not ready for that.

Co: I wouldn't be so afraid of talking about reparation. When you acknowledge that you caused pain, you are being empathic and accepting responsibility. It's like in the Yom Kippur* prayer of self-castigation: "I am guilty, I have betrayed, I have sinned, etc." In the very act of confessing you are making reparation. When you say: "I hurt you badly, I am sorry for the suffering that I caused you," that's already reparation. It's like a marital Yom Kipur.

TH: The problem is that Efi won't budge unless something really shakes him. I don't think that there is enough here to pull him down from the fence.

M5: He can be told: "You know that you are dying a lingering death, that you have no hope, no present and no future . . . "

M4: He must be brought to see that his options are closed because he is disconnected from his feelings. That if he remains so, he will be stuck forever.

The death metaphor refuses to die. Following Lewis Carroll's dictum, "Everything I say three times is true," I overcame my aversion to it and decided to include it in the message.

Co: Let us try it this way: "Why is it worthwhile for you two to strive for these goals? It is worthwhile because both of you are stricken with paralysis. You, Efi, are afraid of your father, afraid of what will happen to you, afraid of your shadow. For as long as you stay like that, you are not alive at all. And you, Shira, feel that the best that could happen

*Day of Atonement.

to you is to become a doormat, for as it is, you are nothing. Unless you take the jump, you will stay paralyzed, waiting to be kicked or to get a heart attack. It is not easy to acknowledge openly that you have hurt your wife badly and deeply in turning her into a non-person, and that you have rejected and rebuffed your husband for years and years. You have to go through this if you want to live. You have to go through this if you want to separate. And you have to go through this if you want to stay together."

M6: They should be warned to expect a possible estrangement at home. Then it doesn't show that the therapy is not working.

M4: Right, for the purpose is not to bring them together, but to release them from the paralysis.

Co: (To therapist) This may help you not to feel blamed when they tell you that at home they are estranged.

The new formulation releases the therapist from the role of family savior. She is now equipped to deal with implicit charges about the couple's estrangement at home.

M4: The curse motif should be inserted too.

Co: Let us try: "What happened that you got so caught in this vicious circle of endless mutual hurts? What happened is that you have been crushed by the weight of a family curse." We then describe the curse and say to him: "You, Efi, have been most loyal to the curse. Your father and your brother found a less fanatical solution. Their family life suffered, but they made some sort of arrangement and managed to go on living. Not for you, however, such handy solutions. You must be loyal and faithful to the very letter of the curse. But still, maybe you will be the first to do without a fake arrangement. By recognizing the curse, you may become the first to fight it and escape it." And to Shira, you may say: "You are bound to the curse by keeping your loyalty to your mother's pattern, which was similar to that of Efi's mother. Your daily prayer by which you make obeisance to the curse is: 'I cannot express feelings openly, I cannot be close, I must remain shrunk, detached and cold.' This is your real enemy. This is the enemy of your personal development, that stops you from moving together or apart."

TH: Good! I believe that this will get through to him. Thanks (she signals that for her the consultation is over).*

Unfortunately, the intervention has still not been put to the test. Precisely at this point in the therapy, Efi stopped coming. The therapist weighed whether she should invite him for an extraordinary session, but decided to save the message for a later occasion. Work proceeded with Shira and, although her mood improved and she became more independent, the marital situation remained much as it was. The therapist feels quite sure that Efi will arrive in the near future, and she will be ready for him with the message.

---

*The therapist was given the tape of the consultation so as to piece together the different formulations into one coherent message.

8

CRITICAL INTERVENTIONS

AND THE MODERN ERA

IN PSYCHOTHERAPY

CRITICAL INTERVENTIONS ARE in many respects torchbearers of the modern *Zeitgeist* in psychotherapy. They thrive on the pluralist readiness to speak a variety of languages, they owe their birthright to the loss of a stable direction, and they echo the modern impatience with lengthy cures. In fact, tentative versions of critical interventions have appeared at different times in the history of psychotherapy, but only in the pluralist era have they found a congenial ecology. And as the true children of this era, they mirror its challenges, disappointments, and compromises.

THE PROBLEM OF LANGUAGE

The problem of language and the dream of its solution in modern psychotherapy have been summarized in the title of an article: "From the tower of Babel to the psychotherapeutic Esperanto" (Vasco, 1990*). In the tower of Babel, each school

---

*Unfortunately, the article is available only in Portuguese.

breeds an idiom and each sect a dialect. As for Esperanto, everyone knows how it fared.

Meetings and congresses have been organized between representatives of contrasting orientations in an attempt to bridge the growing diversity. Some of these events have turned into veritable happenings, with huge audiences and intense media coverage. In a humbler but also more fruitful vein, dialogues have been held in quieter settings or in the pages of books, such as Saltzman and Norcross' *Therapy Wars* (1990), which is clearly an instrument of peace. As the proper atmosphere was created, exponents of different approaches began to understand each other, map similarities, and clarify differences. The progress of this ecumenical spirit (London, 1983) in the course of the last decade is well attested by the fact that, though the more recent of these multimeetings have been quite harmonious, earlier attempts often proved premature, leading only to flagrant cacophany (see Wachtel, 1982, for an example).

For a time, people believed that a common language for psychotherapy might be devised. Attempts were made (Norcross, 1987; Ryle, 1978) and committees set up to forward this goal (Wolfe & Goldfried, 1988). Languages, however, are not created by fiat, but develop out of a living give-and-take. In fact, as therapists from different backgrounds began to converse, common terms and rudimentary "market languages" began to surface (Strenger & Omer, 1992). Such are the idioms of narratives, strategies, and interpersonal interactions, on which the critical interventions in this book are based. These three idioms arose simultaneously at various points along the spectrum of therapeutic approaches, redescribing interventions originally conceived in one framework in terms that were comprehensible to another. The critical intervention, however, goes beyond mere utilization of these idioms: being aimed at all three facets at once, it aspires to a local integration between them.

The consultation group grounds this local integrative attempt on a community of reference. Wanting the ballast of an accepted theory, the terms of the critical intervention might remain ethereal and idiosyncratic, but for the people in the group. By its presence and consensus, the group lends backing to the intervention and offers its members a commonality of meaning.

THE SENSE OF DIRECTION

Therapists must have a sense of whence their patients are coming and where they are heading. When there was only one map and one way, the problem of direction did not arise: one might get stuck, but never lost. Not so present-day therapists, with their many maps and shifting norths. Maybe movement is so important for the modern therapist because rolling along keeps the therapy from faltering. Loss of momentum leads to loss of balance, and stagnation to wobbling and baffling confusion.

Our local goals are not only less abiding than those of yore, but also less inspiring of crusading zeal. "Full self-awareness," "organismic experiencing," "total self-control" — these were goals to kindle a missionary spirit. One hears less and less of their like. Critical interventions fit well with this new state of mind. They rest on the assumption that therapists are ready, even eager, to change gears. To therapists of a previous generation, it was demoralizing to give up their lofty goals. Relinquishing a small goal and its small strategy causes smaller pain. In a monolithic structure, a crack in the wall threatens the whole edifice; in a colony of small dwellings, it involves at most a change of rooms.

THE SHORTENING OF THERAPY

Modern interest in brief forms of psychotherapy is linked to this change in aims. A goal that is devoid of absolute value is not worth pursuing for an eternity. The critical intervention reflects this impatient spirit. Traditionally, psychotherapy used to view quick change as illusory; today it tends to equate slow change with stagnation. Critical interventions are attempts to stir up what we are quick to label as unbearable stillness.

Multiple dialects, small goals, and short breath: what a disillusioned psychotherapy! Many of the profession's great achievements would have never been reached under such an ethos. The old schools of psychotherapy could boast of heroic ventures that could not have come to harbor but for their unwavering faith. Such prowesses of endurance as long-term behavior treatment of autistic children (40,000 hours of training!), medication-free therapeutic milieus for psychotic patients, and quasi-millenarian therapeutic communities for drug-addicts, to name but a few epoch-making enterprises,* could hardly have arisen in our jumpy era.

Not for us such pertinacity. We are bound for other journeys, different joys. We have left the sterling purity of absolute theoretical languages for the helter-skelter and the noise of the open market. There are plenty of flavors and tastes to sample in the market, but our delights are not as enduring as the ones that could be savoured in the palace of knowledge. Compared to our predecessors, we live in theoretical shabbiness, but at least we are not isolated from other ways of thinking and doing. Through windows and cracks in the walls, we exchange views and voices. When we were still green to the infinite variety of the pluralist world, we would, like pampered children, throw away one toy for another that caught our eye. As we matured, however, we developed a new strictness and professional pride: not *anything* goes and no shift is undertaken just for the heck of it. In this book we have seen how a rigorous process of gradual construction and perfecting can take place within a pluralist community. Lacking the permanent abode of a fixed school, modern therapists with their interventions can still enjoy, through and within the crucible of the peer group, a local habitation and a seasonal truth.

---

*It is, however, the bane of school-based psychotherapy that the value of these projects is often acknowledged only within their schools of origin.

Appendix

A FOLLOW-UP OF FORTY THERAPIES
AFTER CONSULTATION

FORTY CONSECUTIVE THERAPIES that had been brought to consultation were followed-up by a semi-structured interview with their respective therapists from six to twelve months after the consultation had taken place. The interview was conducted by an independent investigator previously unacquainted with the therapists. The main purpose of the follow-up was to find out whether: (a) the critical message had been delivered verbatim or with relatively small modifications, with considerable modifications, or not at all; (b) the intervention had resolved the impasse; (c) the themes developed in the critical message remained central to the therapy that developed in its wake; and (d) the client's symptoms or problems improved in the wake of the critical intervention.

The findings on these questions were: (a) in 7 (17.5%) cases the critical message was delivered verbatim or with very small modifications; in 29 (72.5%) cases it was delivered with considerable modifications, each therapist adapting the message to his or her own style and to the pace and development of the session; in 4 (10%) cases it was not delivered; (b) in 28 (70%) cases the therapists felt that the impasse had been resolved and the therapy had moved on to other issues; in 12 (30%) cases the impasse remained; (c) in 27 (67.5%) cases, the therapists reported that the themes developed in the critical message had remained central to the therapy, often in the very terms that were used in the message; (d) in 25 (62.5%) cases the therapists reported that the clients improved and that in their opinion the improvement was related to the critical intervention and to the normal therapy that developed in its wake.

This is a subjective survey, not an objective outcome study. However, keeping in mind that the primary client of consultation is the therapist, his or her opinion and report are clearly relevant. A more objective investigation should be based on recordings of the critical session and subsequent ones, and on objective assessments of the patient's functioning. As it is, this survey should be considered as an exploratory pilot.

REFERENCES

Alexander, F., & French, T. M. (1946). *Psychoanalytic therapy, principles and applications.* New York: Ronald Press.

Bateson, G. (1972a). *Steps to an ecology of mind.* New York: Ballantine.

Bateson, G. (1972b). Bali: The value system of a steady state. In G. Bateson, *Steps to an ecology of mind.* New York: Ballantine.

Beutler, L. E. (1986). Systematic eclectic psychotherapy. In J. C. Norcross (Ed.), *Handbook of eclectic psychotherapy.* New York: Brunner/Mazel.

Bollas, C. (1987). *The shadow of the object: Psychoanalysis of the unthought known.* New York: Columbia University Press.

Boscolo, L., Cecchin, G., Hoffman, L., & Penn, P. (1987). *Milan systemic family therapy.* New York: Basic Books.

Bruner, J. (1986). *Actual minds, possible worlds.* Cambridge, MA: Harvard University Press.

Budman, S. H., & Gurman, A. S. (1988). *Theory and practice of brief therapy.* New York: Guilford.

Butler, S. F., & Strupp, H. H. (1986). Specific and nonspecific factors in psychotherapy: A problematic paradigm for psychotherapy research. *Psychotherapy, 23,* 30–40.

Cornsweet, C. (1983). Nonspecific factors and theoretical choice. *Psychotherapy, 20,* 307–313.

Crits-Christoph, P., Barber, J. P., & Kurcias, J. C. (1993). The accuracy of therapist's interpretations and the development of the therapeutic alliance. *Psychotherapy Research, 3,* 23–35.

DaVerona, M., & Omer, H. (1993). Understanding and countering chronic processes with mental patients: An interpersonal model. *Psychotherapy, 29,* 355–365.

Driscoll, R. (1984). *Pragmatic psychotherapy.* New York: Van Nostrand Reinhold.

Ellis, A. (1962). *Reason and emotion in psychotherapy.* New York: Lyle Stuart.

Fisch, R., Weakland, J. H., & Segal, L. (1982). *The tactics of change: Doing therapy briefly.* San Francisco: Jossey-Bass.

Frank, J. D. (1961/1973). *Persuasion and healing: A comparative study of psychotherapy.* Baltimore: Johns Hopkins University Press.

Frank, J. D. (1987). Psychotherapy, rhetoric, and hermeneutics: Implications for practice and research. *Psychotherapy, 24,* 293–302.

Frankl, V. (1963). *Man's search for meaning.* Boston: Beacon Press.

Gergen, K. J., & Gergen, M. M. (1986). Narrative form and the construction of psychological science. In T. R. Sarbin (Ed.), *Narrative psychology: The storied nature of human conduct.* New York: Praeger.

Gustafson, J. P. (1986). *The complex secret of brief psychotherapy.* New York: Norton.

Gustafson, J. P. (1992). *Self-delight in a harsh world.* New York: Norton.

Haley, J. (1973). *Uncommon therapy: The psychiatric techniques of Milton H. Erickson, M.D.* New York: Norton.

Haley, J. (1984). *Ordeal therapy.* San Francisco: Jossey-Bass.

Haley, J. (1990). *Strategies of psychotherapy* (2nd ed.). Rockville, MD: Triangle Press.

Henry, W. P., Schacht, T. E., & Strupp, H. H. (1986). Structural analysis of social behavior: Application to a study of interpersonal process in differential psychotherapeutic outcome. *Journal of Consulting and Clinical Psychology, 54,* 27–31.

Hoffman, S., & Laub, B. (1986). Paradoxical intervention using a polarization model of cotherapy in the treatment of elective mutism: A case study. *Contemporary Family Therapy, 8,* 136–143.

Horvath, A., & Symond, D. B. (1991). Relation between working alliance and outcome in psychotherapy. *Journal of Counseling Psychology, 38,* 139–143.

Kanfer, F. H., & Scheffe, B. K. (1988). *Guiding the process of therapeutic change.* Champaign, IL: Research Press.

Kazdin, A. E. (1979). Fictions, factions, and functions of behavior therapy. *Behavior Therapy, 10,* 629–654.

Kiesler, D. J. (1982). Interpersonal theory for personality and psychotherapy. In J. C. Anchin & D. J. Kiesler (Eds.), *Handbook of interpersonal psychotherapy.* Elmsford, NY: Pergamon Press.

Kiesler, D. J. (1983). The 1982 interpersonal circle: A taxonomy for complementarity in human transactions. *Psychological Review, 90,* 185–214.

Krantz, S. E. (1985). When depressive cognitions reflect negative realities. *Cognitive Therapy and Research, 9,* 595–610.

Kübler-Ross, E. (1969). *On death and dying.* New York: Macmillan.

Kuhn, T. (1962). *The structure of scientific revolution.* Chicago: University of Chicago Press.

Lange, A. (1989). The "help" paradigm in the treatment of severely distressed couples: A combination of paradoxical and problem-solving elements. *American Journal of Family Therapy, 17,* 3–13.

Lange, A., & Omer, H. (1991). Wirkung und Inhalt: Die zwei Seiten therapeutischer Interventionen. *Praxis der Psychotherapie und Psychosomatik, 36,* 117–131.

Lazarus, A. A. (1971). *Behavior therapy and beyond.* New York: McGraw-Hill.

Lazarus, A. A. (1977). Has behavior therapy outlived its usefulness? *American Psychologist, 32,* 550–554.

Lazarus, A. A. (1989). *The practice of multimodal therapy.* Baltimore: Johns Hopkins University Press.

London, P. (1972). The end of ideology in behavior modification. *American Psychologist, 27,* 913–920.

London, P. (1983). Ecumenism in psychotherapy. *Contemporary Psychology, 28,* 507–508.

London, P. (1986). *The modes and morals of psychotherapy* (2nd ed.). New York: McGraw-Hill.

Luborsky, L. (1984). *Principles of psychoanalytic psychotherapy: A manual for supportive-expressive treatment.* New York: Basic Books.

Luborsky, L., Singer, B., & Luborsky, L. (1975). Comparative studies of psychotherapies: Is it true that "Everybody has won and all must have prizes?" *Archives of General Psychiatry, 32,* 995–1008.

Mahoney, M. J. (1980). Psychotherapy and the structure of personal revolutions. In M. J. Mahoney (Ed.), *Psychotherapy Process* (pp. 157–179). New York: Plenum.

Mann, J. (1973). *Time-limited psychotherapy.* Cambridge, MA: Harvard University Press.

Mann, J. (1981). The core of time-limited psychotherapy: Time and the central issue. In S. H. Budman (Ed.), *Forms of brief therapy.* New York: Guilford.

Meichenbaum, D., & Gilmore, J. B. (1984). The nature of unconscious processes: A cognitive behavioral perspective. In K. S. Bowers & D. Meichenbaum (Eds.), *The unconscious reconsidered.* New York: Wiley.

Messer, S. B. (1986). Eclecticism in psychotherapy: Underlying assumptions, problems, and trade-offs. In J. C. Norcross (Ed.), *Handbook of eclectic psychotherapy.* New York: Brunner/Mazel.

Messer, S. B., Sass, L. A., & Woolfolk, R. L. (Eds.). (1988). *Hermeneutics and psychological theory: Interpretive perspectives on personality, psy-*

chotherapy, and psychopathology. New Brunswick, NJ: Rutgers University Press.

Minuchin, S. (1974). *Families and family therapy*. Cambridge, MA: Harvard University Press.

Norcross, J. C. (1986). Eclectic psychotherapy: An introduction and overview. In J. C. Norcross (Ed.), *Handbook of Eclectic Psychotherapy*. New York: Brunner/Mazel.

Norcross, J. C. (1987). Toward a common language for psychotherapy: An introduction. *Journal of Integrative and Eclectic Psychotherapy*, 6, 180–184.

Norcross, J. C. (1990). Commentary: Eclecticism misrepresented and integration misunderstood. *Psychotherapy*, 27, 297–300.

Omer, H. (1987). Therapeutic impact: A nonspecific major factor in directive psychotherapies. *Psychotherapy*, 24, 52–57.

Omer, H. (1989). Specifics and nonspecifics in psychotherapy. *American Journal of Psychotherapy*, 43, 181–192.

Omer, H. (1990). Enhancing the impact of therapeutic interventions. *American Journal of Psychotherapy*, 44, 218–231.

Omer, H. (1991a). Writing a post-scriptum to a badly ended therapy. *Psychotherapy*, 28, 484–492.

Omer, H. (1991b). Dialectical interventions and the structure of strategy. *Psychotherapy*, 28, 563–571.

Omer, H. (1992). Theoretical, empirical, and clinical foundations of the concept of "therapeutic impact." *Journal of Psychotherapy Integration*, 2, 193–206.

Omer, H. (1993a). The integrative focus: Coordinating symptom- and person-oriented perspectives in therapy. *American Journal of Psychotherapy*, 47, 283–295.

Omer, H. (1993b). Quasi-literary elements in psychotherapy. *Psychotherapy*, 30, 59–66.

Omer, H. (in press). Short-term psychotherapy and the rise of the life-sketch. *Psychotherapy*.

Omer, H., & Alon, N. (1989). Principles of psychotherapeutic strategy. *Psychotherapy*, 28, 282–289.

Omer, H., & Alon, N. (in press). The continuity principle: A unified approach to disaster and trauma. *American Journal of Community Psychology*.

Omer, H., Dar, R., Weiner, B., & Grossbard, O. (in press). A process scale for impact promoting activities. *Journal of Psychotherapy Research*.

Omer, H., Kadmon, A., Wiseman, H., & Dar, R. (1992). Therapeutic impact in smoking cessation: Accounting for the differential effectiveness of treatments. *Psychotherapy*, 29, 653–659.

Omer, H., & London, P. (1988). Metamorphosis in psychotherapy: The end of the systems' era. *Psychotherapy*, 25, 171–180.

Omer, H., & Strenger, C. (1992). From the one true meaning to an infinity of constructed ones. *Psychotherapy*, 29, 253–261.

Perls, F. (1969). *Gestalt therapy verbatim*. New York: Wiley.

Rabkin, R. (1977). *Strategic psychotherapy*. New York: Basic Books.

Rachman, S. (1980). Emotional processing. *Behaviour Research and Therapy, 18*, 51–60.

Russel, R. L., & van den Broek, P. (1992). Changing narrative schemas in psychotherapy. *Psychotherapy, 29*, 344–354.

Ryle, A. A. (1978). A common language for the psychotherapies? *British Journal of Psychiatry, 132*, 585–594.

Safran, J. D. (in press). Breaches in the therapeutic alliance: An arena for negotiating authentic relatedness. *Psychotherapy*.

Safran, J. D., Crocker, P., McMain, S., & Murray, P. (1990). Therapeutic alliance rupture as a therapeutic event for empirical investigation. *Psychotherapy, 27*, 154–165.

Saltzman, N., & Norcross, J. C. (Eds.). (1990). *Therapy wars*. San Francisco: Jossey-Bass.

Sarbin, T. R. (1986). *Narrative psychology: The storied nature of human conduct*. New York: Praeger.

Schafer, R. (1982). *The analytic attitude*. New York: Basic Books.

Smith, M. L., Glass, G. V., & Miller, T. I. (1980). *The benefits of psychotherapy*. Baltimore: Johns Hopkins University Press.

Spence, D. (1982). *Narrative truth and historical truth: Meaning and interpretation in psychoanalysis*. New York: Norton.

Spence, D. (1983). Narrative persuasion. *Psychoanalysis and Contemporary Thought, 6*, 457–481.

Spence, D. (1987). *The Freudian metaphor*. New York: Norton.

Standal, S. W., & Corsini, R. J. (1959). *Critical incidents in psychotherapy*. Englewood Cliffs, NJ: Prentice-Hall.

Strenger, C., & Omer, H. (1992). Pluralist criteria for psychotherapeutic interventions: An alternative to sectarianism, anarchy, and utopian integration. *American Journal of Psychotherapy, 46*, 111–130.

Strupp, H. H., & Binder, J. L. (1984). *Psychotherapy in a new key: A guide to time-limited dynamic psychotherapy*. New York: Basic Books.

Talmon, M. (1990). *Single session therapy*. San Francisco: Jossey-Bass.

Tomm, K. (1984a). One perspective on the Milan systemic approach: Part I. Overview of development, theory and practice. *Journal of Marital and Family Therapy, 10*, 113–125.

Tomm, K. (1984b). One perspective on the Milan systemic approach: Part II. Description of session format, interviewing style and interventions. *Journal of Marital and Family Therapy, 10*, 253–271.

Vasco, A. B. (1990). Da torre de Babel ao esperanto terapeutico [From the tower of Babel to the psychotherapeutic Esperanto]. *Psiquiatria Clinica, 11*, 117–123.

Wachtel, P. L. (Ed.). (1982). *Resistance: Psychodynamic and behavioral approaches*. New York: Plenum.

Watzlawick, P., Weakland, J. H., & Fisch, R. (1974). *Change: Principles of problem formation and problem resolution*. New York: Norton.

White, M., & Epston, D. (1990). *Narrative means to therapeutic ends.* New York: Norton.

Wolfe, B. E., & Goldfried, M. R. (1988). Research on psychotherapy integration: Recommendations and conclusions from an NIMH workshop. *Journal of Consulting and Clinical Psychology, 56,* 448–451.

Yalom, I. (1980). *Existential psychotherapy.* New York: Basic Books.

INDEX

163